Every. Now. Then.

Every. Now. Then.
Reframing Nationhood

Edited by Andrew Hunter

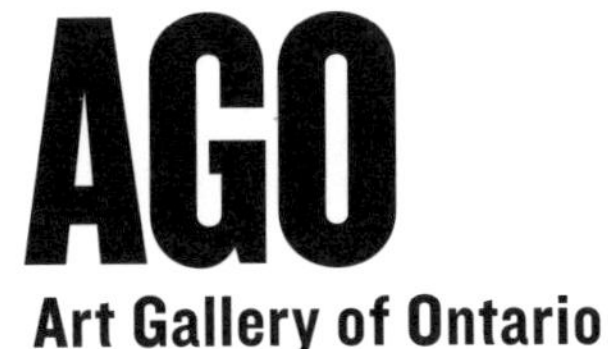

The Art Gallery of Ontario operates on land that has been a site of human activity for over 15,000 years. This land has been the territory of the Huron-Wendat and Petun First Nations, the Seneca, and the Anishinaabe. The Dish with One Spoon Wampum Belt Covenant is an agreement between the Iroquois Confederacy and the Anishinaabe Three Fires Confederacy to peaceably share and care for the resources around the Great Lakes. Toronto is also governed by a treaty between the federal government of Canada and the Mississaugas of New Credit, known as the Toronto Purchase. Toronto has always been a trading centre for First Nations.

Works

Essays

Director's Foreword

Canada 150—the sesquicentennial of Canada's confederation—is a complex moment in the history of this young nation, a moment both celebrated and contested. As a leading public art museum, the Art Gallery of Ontario has a unique opportunity and responsibility to engage with this moment. Through the curatorial and artistic vision of *Every. Now. Then: Reframing Nationhood,* we aim to be a place of dialogue, reflection, and exchange; to make a lasting contribution to this national conversation; and to reframe the narrative of art and nationhood in Canada.

At its core, the exhibition *Every. Now. Then.* is a presentation of extraordinary works of art by a group of talented artists—many of whom have produced new work specifically for this occasion. Both the exhibition and this accompanying publication are grounded in strong Indigenous perspectives, as well as voices from Canada's diverse migrant populations, including Black communities. My hope is that this exhibition will contribute to more complex and inclusive narratives of Canadian nationhood and art history.

It is with immense gratitude that I thank all of the artists in *Every. Now. Then,* for sharing with us their excellent work. I also offer my sincere thanks to the curatorial team, led by Andrew Hunter (the AGO's Fredrik S. Eaton Curator, Canadian Art), with the collaboration of Anique Jordan and Quill Christie-Peters. Working alongside them has been an outstanding exhibition team, without whom none of the AGO's exhibitions would be realized. My appreciation is also extended to the staff of the Art Gallery of Ontario, who, in each of their roles, have made *Every. Now. Then.* possible. This exhibition has been generously supported by our government partners: Ontario 150, the Government of Canada, and the Canada Council for the Arts.

Finally, this publication includes a series of powerful writings and I am grateful to the writers, Quill Christie-Peters, Rachelle Dickenson, Anique Jordan, Srimoyee Mitra, Charmaine A. Nelson, Rosie Spooner, and Andrew Hunter, along with editor Mosa McNeilly, for their valuable insights.

Stephan Jost
Michael and Sonja Koerner Director, and CEO
Art Gallery of Ontario

Curator's Introduction

What does Canada mean in 2017, and what potential transformative potential does the country's sesquicentennial birthday offer? Celebrated by many as Canada 150, 2017 is equally being challenged by many (including the Indigenous-lead protest, #Resistance 150). Those protesting are questioning the country's history as a colonial project that sought to, and seeks to, displace and erase Indigenous peoples, and write out of the national narrative many who fall outside the "founding" cultures of French and English Canada.

From their inception, the exhibition and publication—*Every. Now. Then: Rethinking Nationhood*—have been developed to engage critically with the idea of Canada. They embrace the fundamental belief that this country remains a dynamic work-in-progress that has, is, and will continue to be defined by movements and migrations across shifting terrain and within a variable, often unstable, environment. As cultural space, political state, ecosystem, and geography, the space of Canada (even over its short history) has been a place of shifting borders and boundaries; a place constantly being reimagined and redefined. So what is being celebrated?

Back in 1967, during Canada's last big birthday celebration, there was Expo 67, Montreal's splashy, modern, coming-out party for the centennial of a country that was positioning itself as a progressive, liberal presence on the global stage. The memories of this extravaganza are flush with bold architecture and hip content. At the heart of the fair's innovations was the United States pavilion—a geodesic dome designed by Buckminster Fuller—and Moshe Safdie's new model housing complex, Habitat 67. Canada offered an inverted pyramid as its pavilion. There was a monorail (all world's fairs must have one) and the hosting staff was adorned in surprisingly fashionable attire for Canada in the 1960s. In addition to Canada's main pavilion, there were also buildings for the provinces and territories, as well as for Canadian industry.

Then there was The Indians of Canada pavilion. Designed to emulate a teepee, this pavilion featured two striking murals created by Norval Morrisseau on the interior and exterior of a building that housed exhibits highlighting First Nations, Métis, and Inuit culture. And there was more; something that, in retrospect, seems surprising and unexpected. The Indians of Canada pavilion included the story—told through photographs and text—of Canada's Residential School System; a system initiated by the country's first Prime Minister, Sir John A. Macdonald, and Christian churches through the still extant Indian Act, and operated by Anglican, Roman Catholic, Presbyterian, and United (including Methodist) churches for close to a century. A system impacting over 150,000 youth, their families, communities, and descendants, it was, in fact, still widely in operation in 1967.[1]

It is only now, fifty years on from Expo 67, that Canada has slowly come to admit to this legacy, and to struggle through the problematic process of truth and reconciliation, accountability and healing. This story is a reminder that it takes more than just acknowledgement and inclusion to change; it requires actions. As is so often pointed out, *The Report of the Truth and Reconciliation Commission* of 2016 includes "Calls to Action," not simply "recommendations," and art galleries and museums are explicitly called out to act and be accountable.[2]

Every. Now. Then: Rethinking Nationhood takes the position that the land known as Canada is Indigenous territory, and that what isn't already defined by legally binding treaties remains unceded territory (including the land that this nation's capital occupies). And so, this project places a strong emphasis on Indigenous perspectives along with the inclusion of Black viewpoints, and a diversity of voices offering distinct approaches to history, time, and narrative. Like Canada at this moment, *Every. Now. Then: Rethinking Nationhood* offers more questions than answers; it is complex and, possibly, a little messy.

While offering a condensed record of the exhibition, this publication also includes commissioned writings by Quill Christie-Peters, Rachelle Dickenson, Anique Jordan, Srimoyee Mitra, Charmaine A. Nelson, and Rosie Spooner. Rather than ask this remarkable group of thinkers to write about the exhibition, we asked them to reflect on this moment in Canada. While in some cases specific art works from the exhibition are highlighted, each writer has ultimately expressed ideas that they feel are essential to this moment: ideas of a past we cannot lose, of a present we must comprehend, and of a future we must be accountable to. These writings are complemented by the thoughts and images of all the artists who participated in the exhibition, compiled and edited by Laura Robb, AGO Interpretive Planner.

I am extremely grateful to all of the artists and writers presented here for engaging with a project of this kind at such a precarious moment, and for offering their trust in us at the AGO to live up to our commitment to be open, critical, and self-critical, as we developed this ambitious exhibition. Thanks to the core creative team of Quill Christie-Peters, Anique Jordan, and Laura Robb, who committed to collaborating with me. My understanding of this place and time remains a work-in-progress.

Andrew Hunter
Fredrik S. Eaton Curator, Canadian Art
Art Gallery of Ontario

NOTES

1. J. R. Miller, "Residential Schools: Residential schools were government-sponsored religious schools established to assimilate Indigenous children into Euro-Canadian culture," Historica Canada website, 2012.

2. Truth and Reconciliation Commission of Canada, *Truth and Reconciliation Commission of Canada: Calls to Action* (2015).

Works

Barry Ace

I replicate Great Lakes beadwork floral motifs with electronic capacitors and resistors. There's a beautiful metaphor in there, because the beaded flower is really a medicine flower, and like medicine, when a plant is infused, it releases healing energy. Similarly, capacitors and resistors store, and also release, energy and power. It's a nice parallel between the electronic components and the floral motif.

The suite of bandolier bags show family photographs and a 1925 silent film depicting bureaucrats visiting Manitoulin Island to watch the community perform for them in traditional regalia. The irony is that by 1925 the Indian Act's legislation made regalia and dance illegal. The only reason the community could dance was because of the visiting officials.

trinity suite:
Bandolier for Niibwa Ndanwendaagan (My Relatives);
Bandolier for Manidoo-minising (Manitoulin Island);
Bandolier for Charlie (In Memoriam), 2015
Mixed media, various sizes
Courtesy of the artist
Photo by Earl Truelove

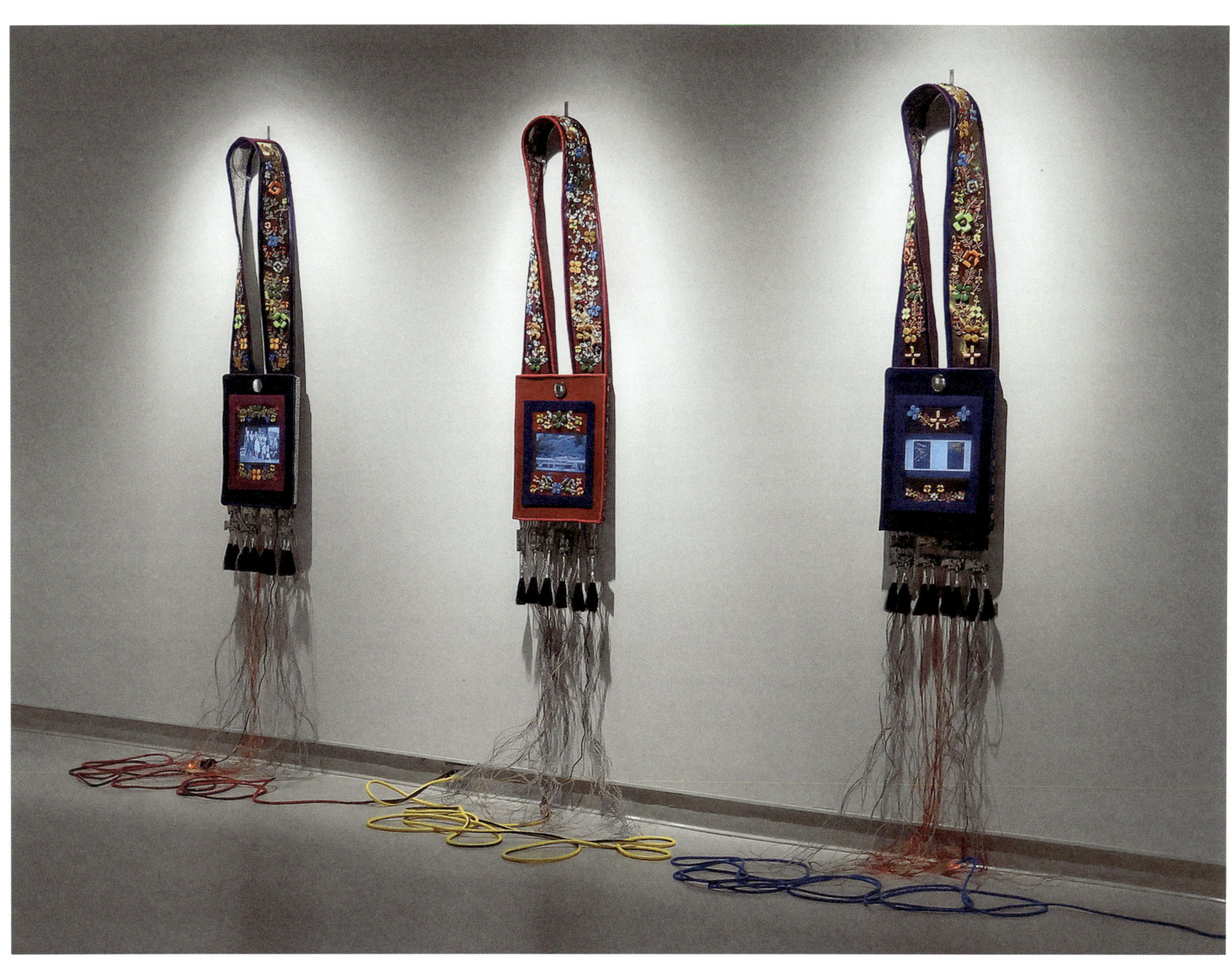

Saimaiyu Akesuk

My parents were not artists and I did not think about making art at all until later. I did know about my grandfather (Latcholasie Akesuk, 1919–2000) and had seen many images of his sculptures… I used to doodle when I went to Arctic College, and Ningeokuluk Teevee (artist, b. 1963) encouraged me to draw. In fact, she took a doodle I did to the Co-op (WBEC, Kinngait/Cape Dorset, around 2012) to show them that I was drawing. When I started, I sometimes thought my grandfather was helping me, because when I could not decide what to draw, I would think of his style of carving. I would look at the paper for ages and remember his works. My first few drawings were doodles and landscapes, but then I started drawing birds and animals. I have to be alone when I draw. Now I am working, teaching at the school, so it is hard. I have a two-year-old boy who takes all my energy. My daughter, Joanne, is the only one who I will let watch me draw. Tim Pitsiulak is my uncle.

Lemmings Buttocks are Dirty, 2013
Coloured pencil on paper, 127 × 81.3 cm
On loan from Karen Schreiber and Marnie Schreiber

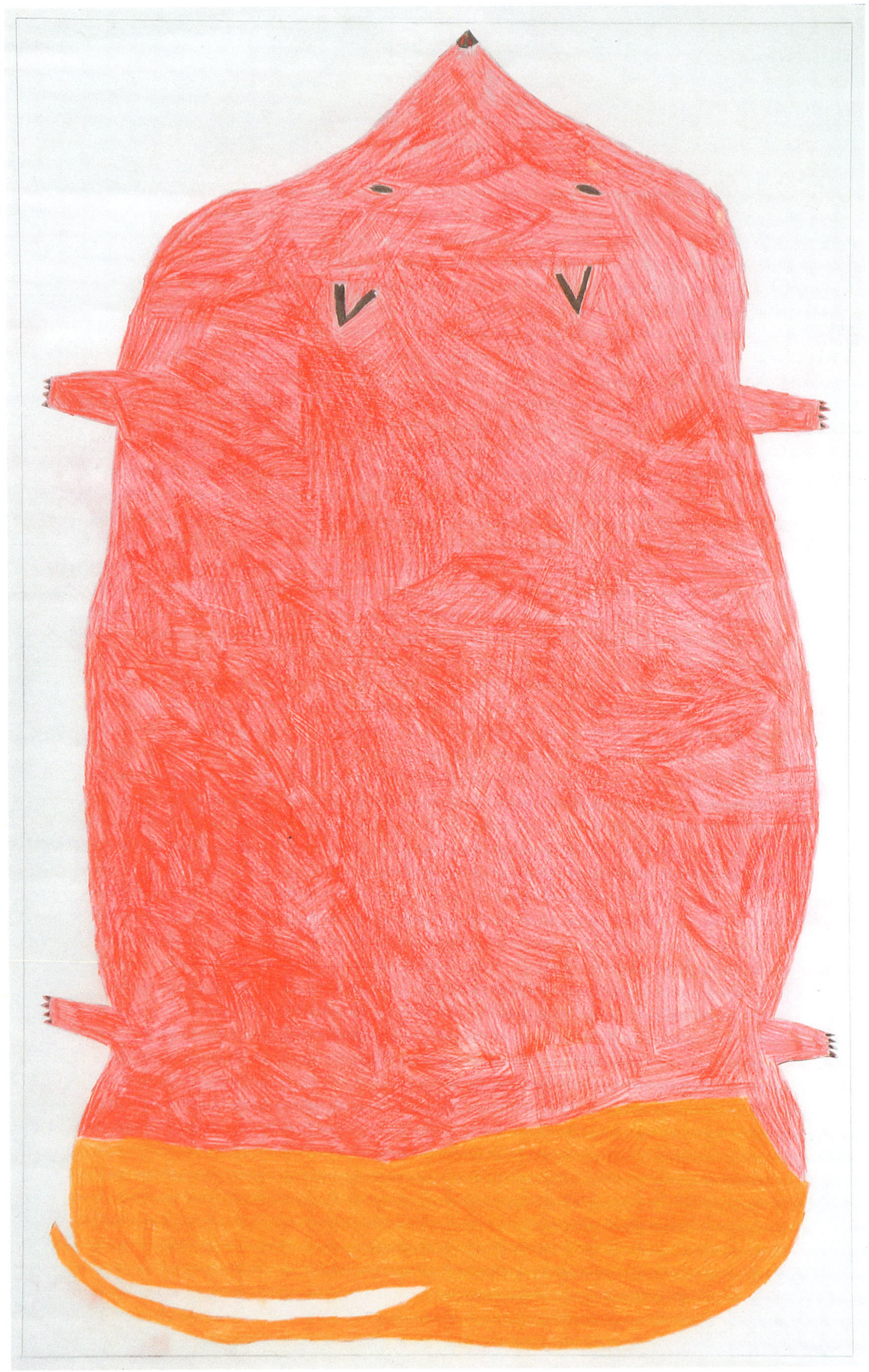

Shuvinai and I stand fixated on the sharply delineated white Arctic peaks of Lawren S. Harris's *Baffin Island*, the type of image that has become an icon of Canada as "Great White North." She wonders aloud, "Where are all the people, where are the animals?" She goes on to describe the giant monster fish that she imagines lingers beneath the waves. "The mountains are Inuktitut," she tells me, "they are my language. They go down into the earth, into the ground, to meet the dead." She smiles, shrugs, and turns away from the painting of Baffin Island, her home. "Why can't they see that?" she whispers.

Andrew Hunter, Fredrik S. Eaton Curator, Canadian Art,
in conversation with Shuvinai Ashoona at the AGO, March 2017

Untitled (Cephalopod), 2016
Coloured pencil and ink on paper, 223.2 × 51 cm
Collection of the Art Gallery of Ontario

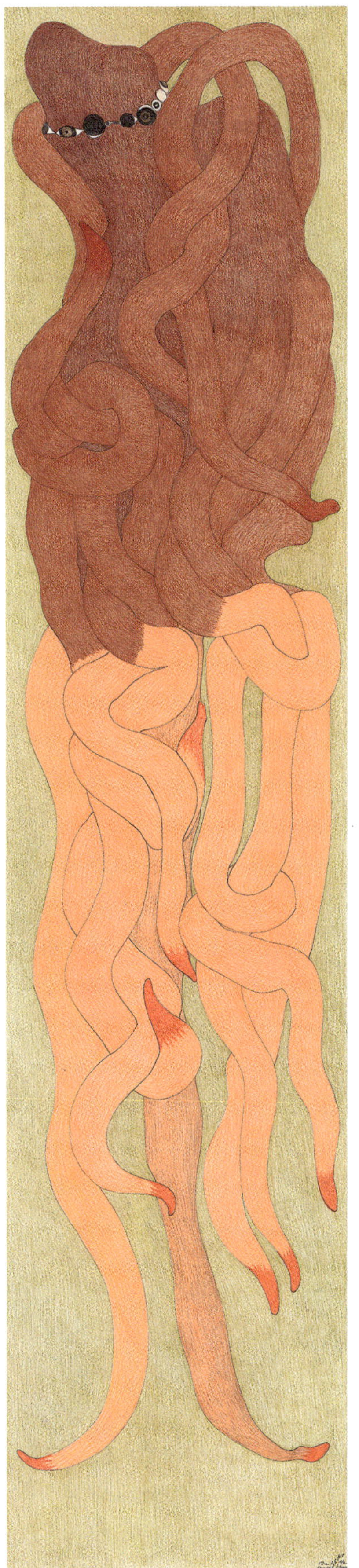

Amalie Atkins

Our consciousness shifts as grief strikes, unfolds, and exists within us; ever present and invisible. Our sense of time changes; we age internally.

Transvection, 2017
Video still from video and sound projection
(from 16mm film transfer), 4:25 minutes, looped
Courtesy of the artist and dc3 Art Projects

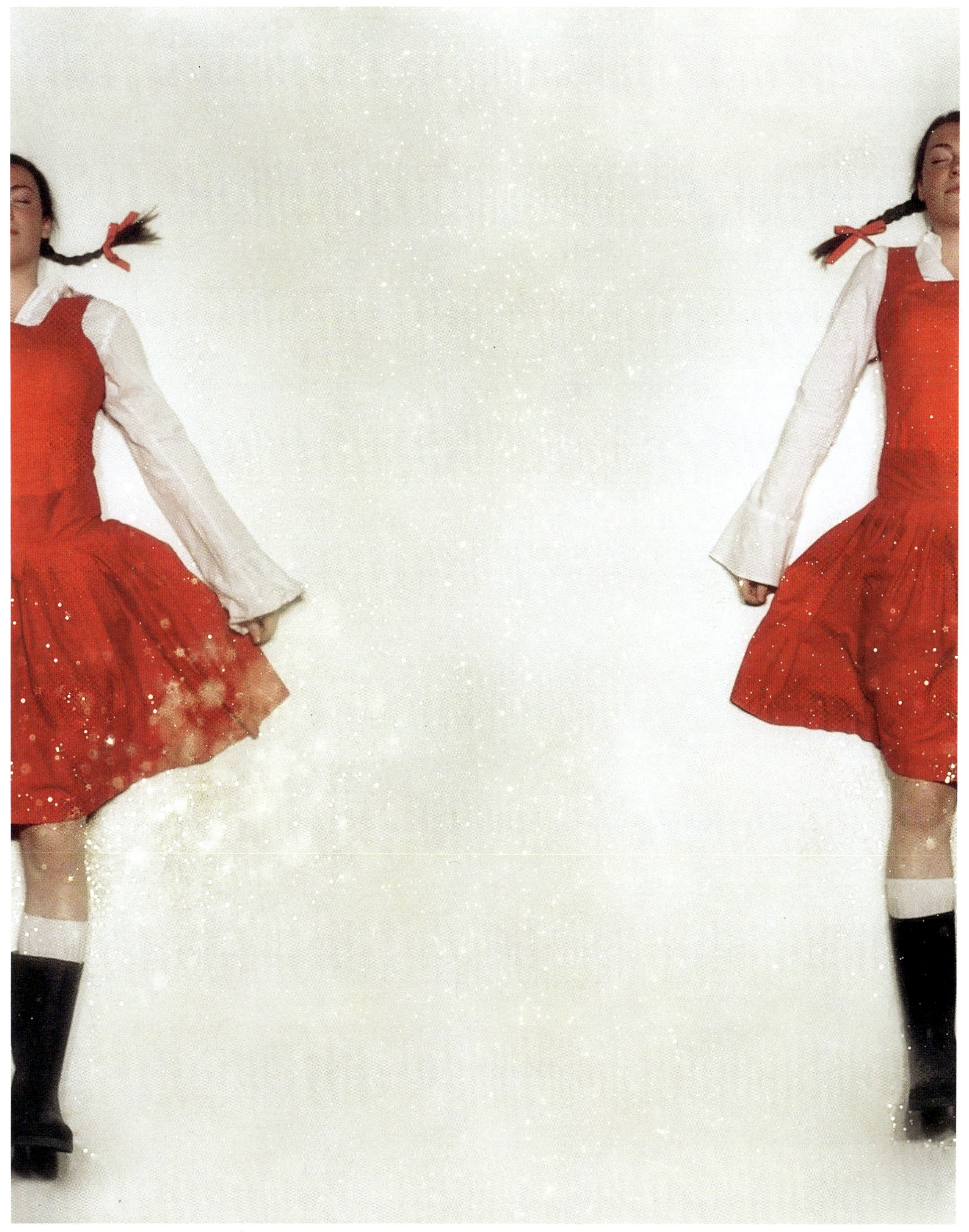

Michael Belmore

For the Anishinaabe, *mishibizhiig* are the underwater panthers, and *animikiig* are the thunderbirds. These manitous, or spirits of the sky and water, have long been enemies. Their conflict results in storms, thunder strikes, and the crashing of waves upon the shore. In their struggle is the power that is nature. For me, *Rumble* is very much about dealing with an Armageddon, and the importance of remembering that nature can make you feel small and fragile.

Rumble, 2017
Copper, wood, aluminium, gouache and LED lights,
172.2 × 147.3 × 24.1 cm
Courtesy of the artist
Photo by Michael Cullen

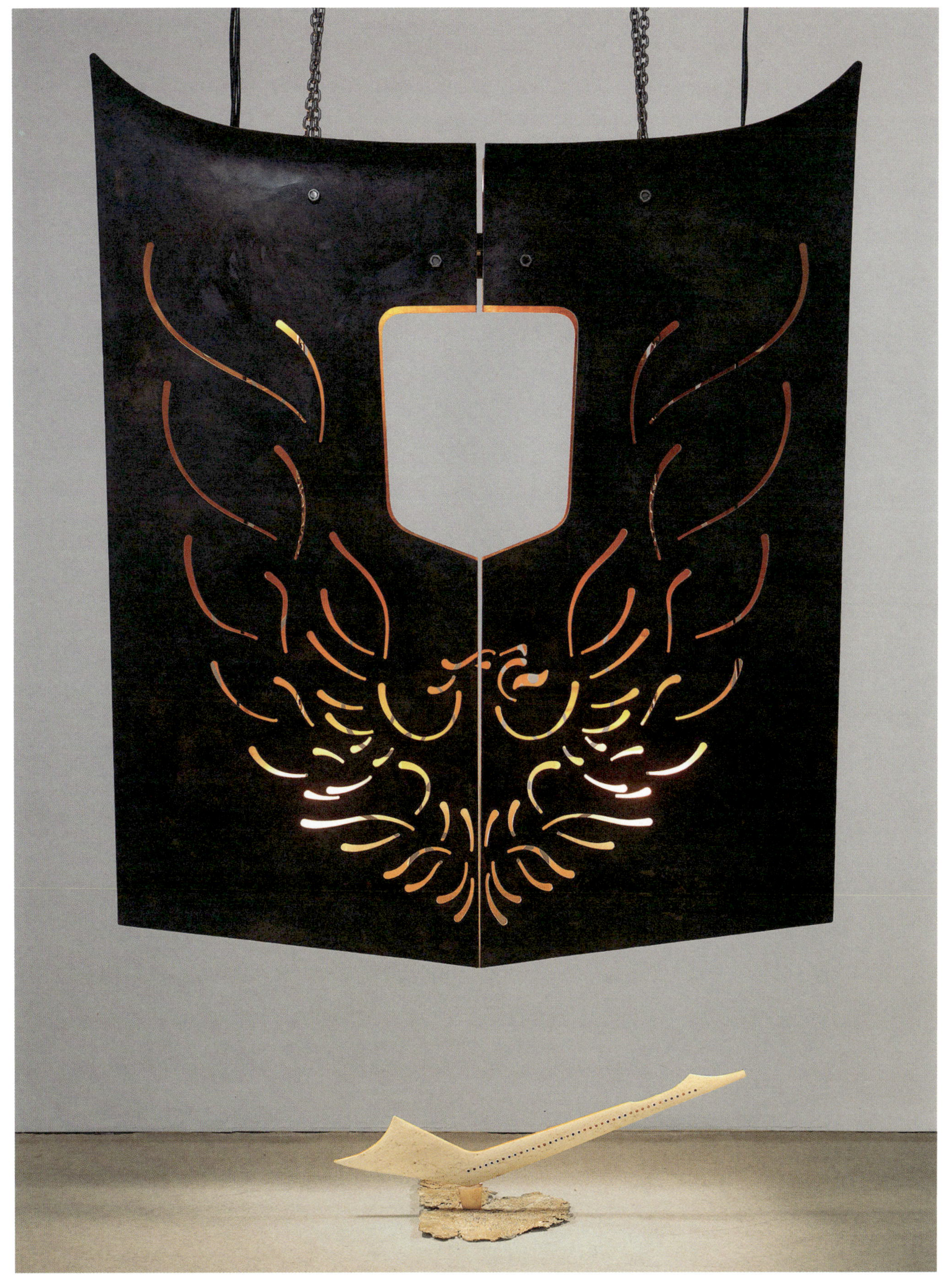

Quill Christie-Peters

I am an Anishinaabekwe arts programmer and self-taught visual artist, and I'm from Treaty 3 territory.* That area has a history of Canadian government-sanctioned flooding. For that reason, people from my community have ended up all across Turtle Island, and largely in urban centres. In turn, city spaces, in their attempts to erase Indigenous people, often try to render the city as non-Indigenous territory.

There are ways for displaced, urban Indigenous people to practice accountability both to the territories they reside on and to their homelands. I work with youth, and I try to give them the knowledge of how settler colonialism operates spatially to remove Indigenous bodies and minds from Indigenous homelands. In this sense, in this work, we reject shame as something that is perpetuated and operationalized as a colonial objective.

*Treaty 3 covers Ontario's northwestern corner, edging into Manitoba.

mitanjigaamiing, 2016
Digital photograph, dimensions variable
Courtesy of the artist

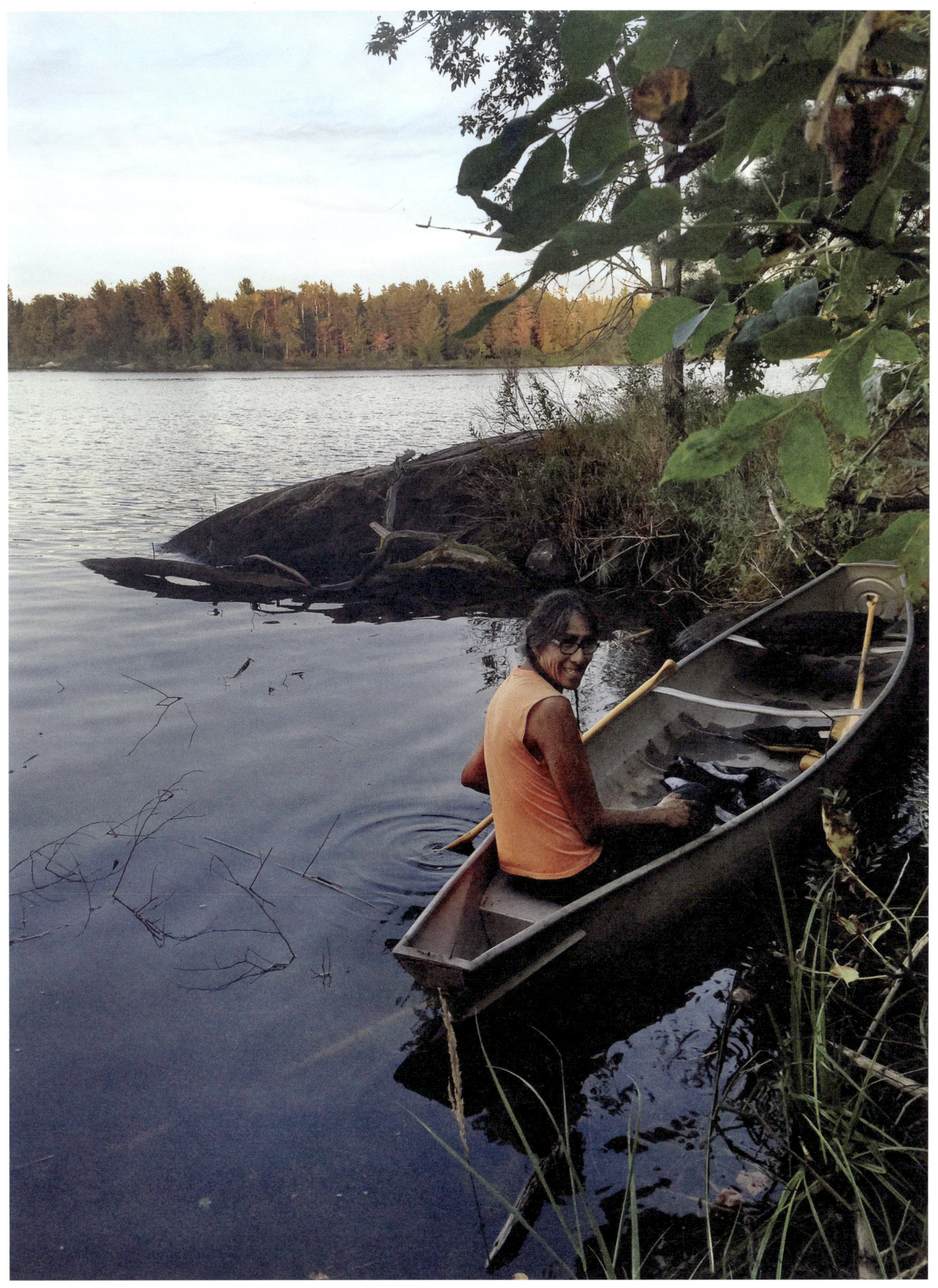

November 13, 2011: Attawapiskat First Nation declared a housing emergency. Black mould was found in the houses. When we watch "Holmes on Homes," rooms with black mould are blocked off from the rest of the house. People in contamination suits come in, bag the mouldy drywall, and treat the area. The images of shacks built by Band members, some with blue tarps as roofs, have stayed with me.

I am alarmed by the contaminated water issues that many First Nation communities across Canada face. These beaded magnified bacterium and parasites are found in the ninety-four First Nations that currently have boil water advisories.

Don't Breathe, Don't Drink, 2016
94 vessels with glass beads and resin, hand-beaded blue tarpaulin tablecloth, and gas board, dimensions variable
Collection of the Art Gallery of Ontario, purchase, with funds from Karen Schreiber and Marnie Schreiber through The American Friends of the Art Gallery of Ontario, Inc., 2017, 2016/432
Photo courtesy of the artist and dc3 Art Projects

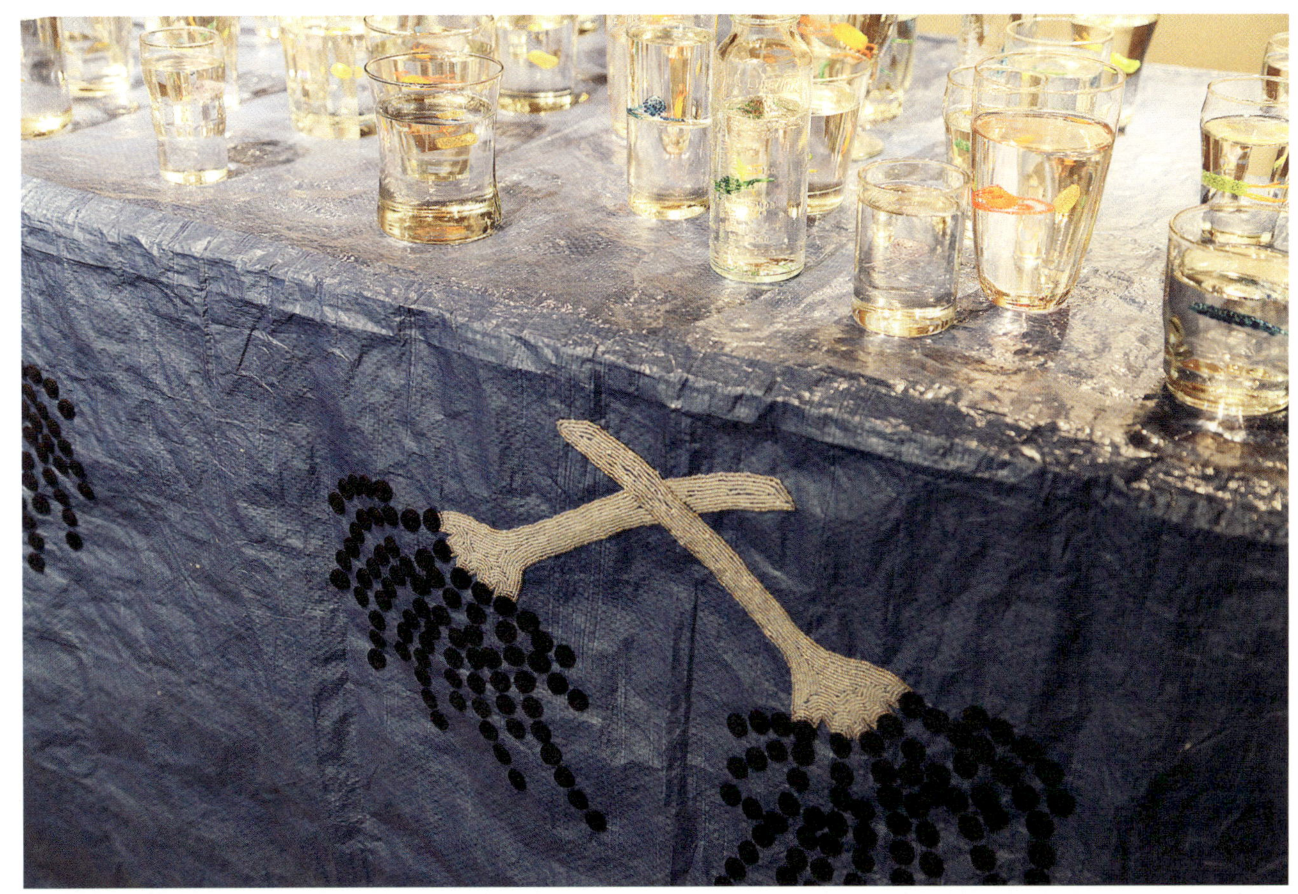

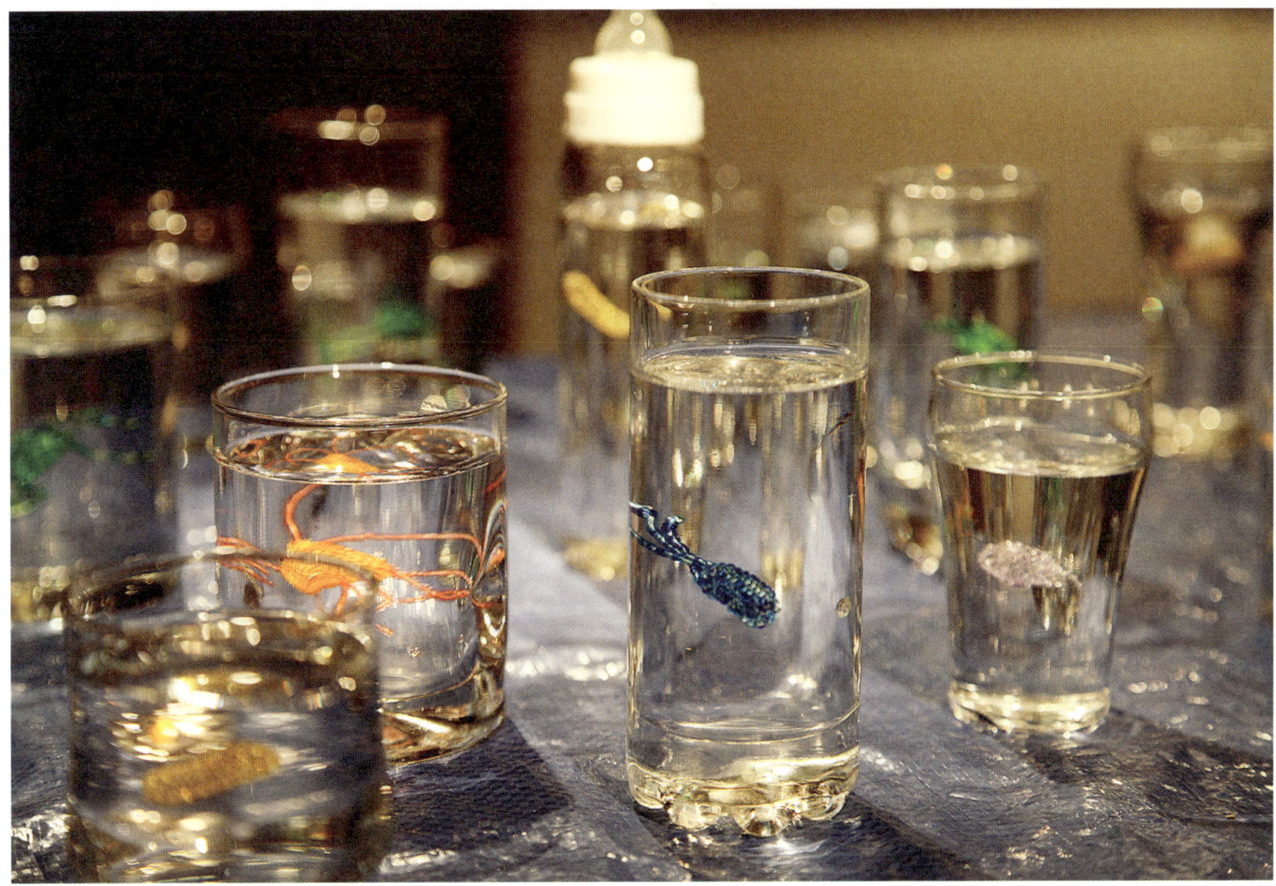

Bonnie Devine

I think it's time that we think about how multi-dimensional and complex our history is, and make room for other voices, other narratives, and other perspectives.

Anishinaabitude, from my installation *Battle for the Woodlands,* represents the Ojibwe of Serpent River First Nation, the Anishinaabe of Walpole Island First Nation, and the Misi-zaagiing of the Mississaugas of the New Credit First Nation. I made the figures by weaving living branches gathered in each location with commercially available seagrass, as a reminder of our enduring presence on this land.

Anishinaabitude, 2016
Maple, red willow, unidentified twigs, paper, and seagrass,
three figures, 224 × 89 × 107 cm, 229 × 33 × 44 cm, 229 × 17 × 153 cm
Collection of the Art Gallery of Ontario, purchase, with funds from
Karen Schreiber and Marnie Schreiber through The American Friends
of the Art Gallery of Ontario, Inc., 2017, 2016/168

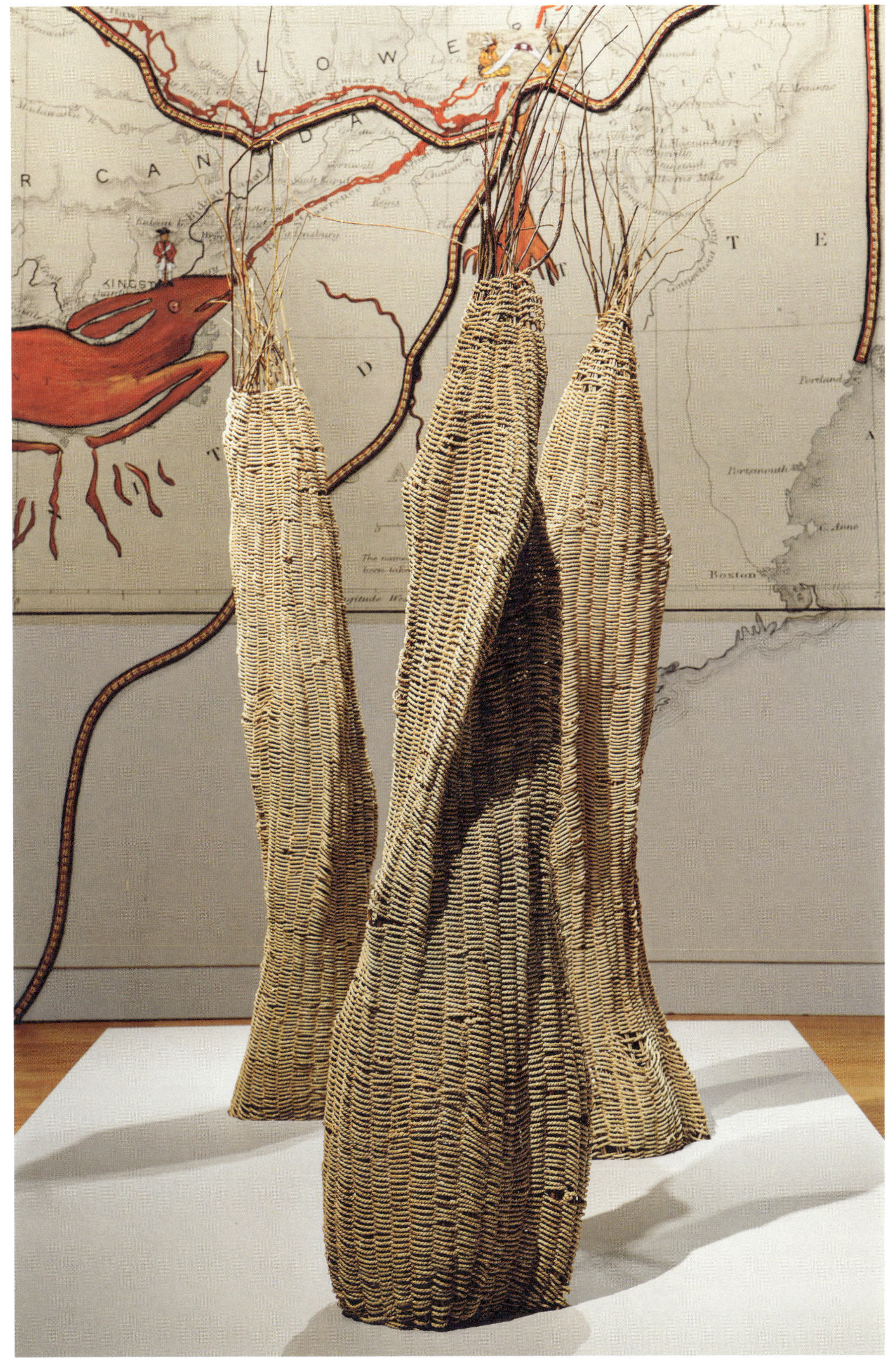
Portland
Portsmouth
C. Anne
Boston

Rosalie Favell

I'm trying to illustrate what we looked like as a Métis family in the 1960s. People often say, "That looks just like my snapshots, our family snapshots." Yeah, that's what we looked like.

My sister and I used to wear our watches really tight so that we could pull it back and say, "See? We're not that dark, it's a tan." Culturally ingrained racism affected my upbringing.

From an Early Age – Revisited: First Day, Clear Lake, Family, Hunting Party (from top left, clockwise), 2015–2016
Oil on canvas, four paintings, 61 × 61 cm each
Courtesy of the artist

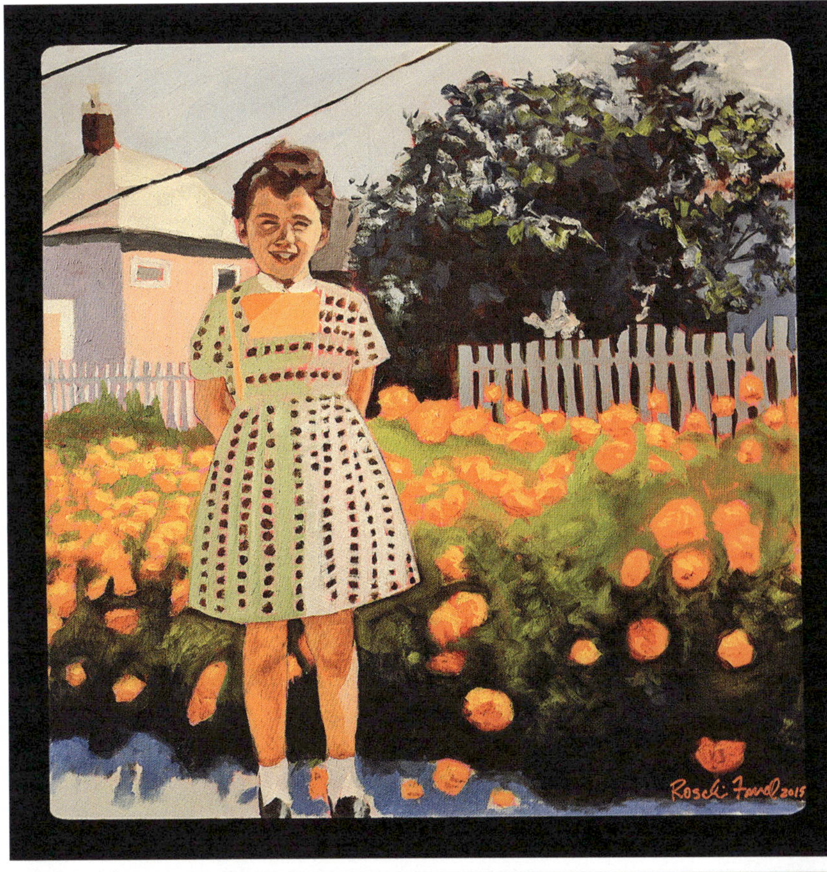

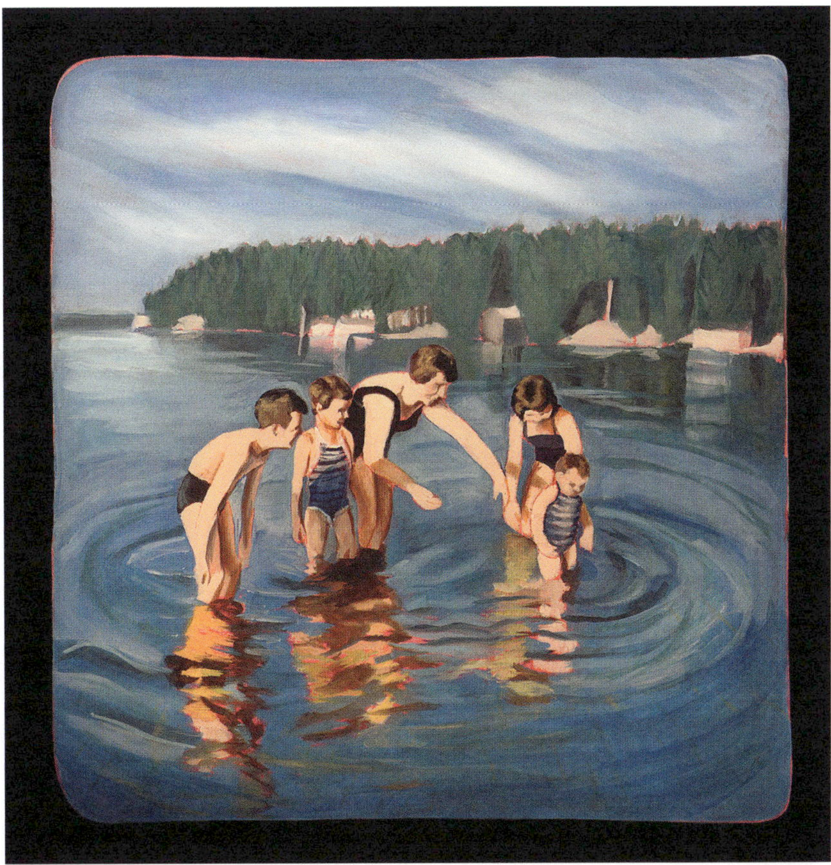

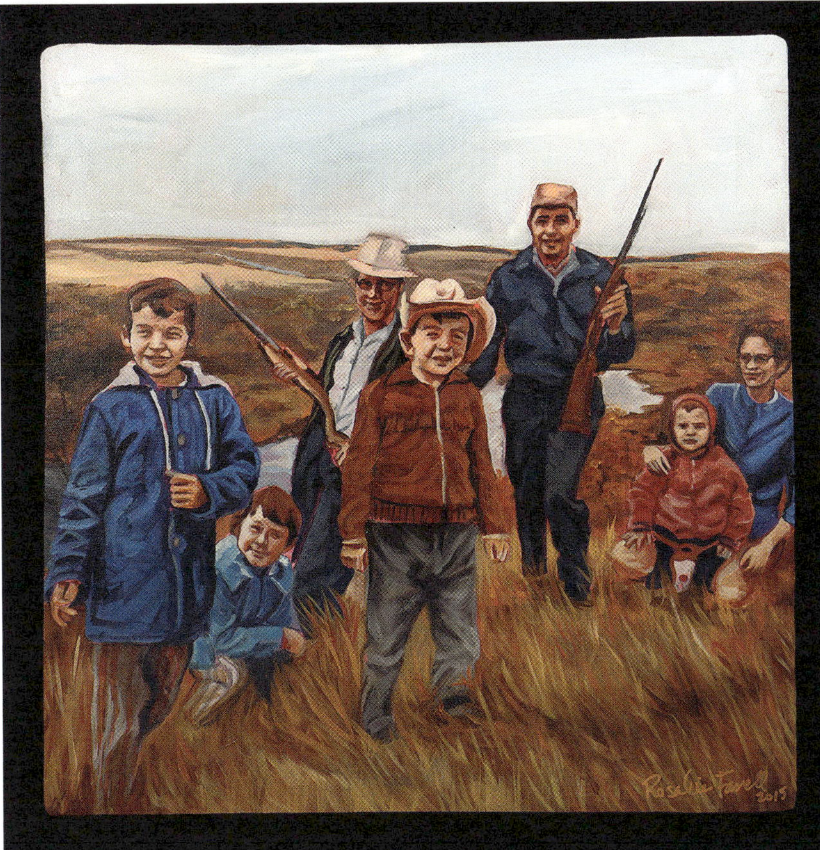

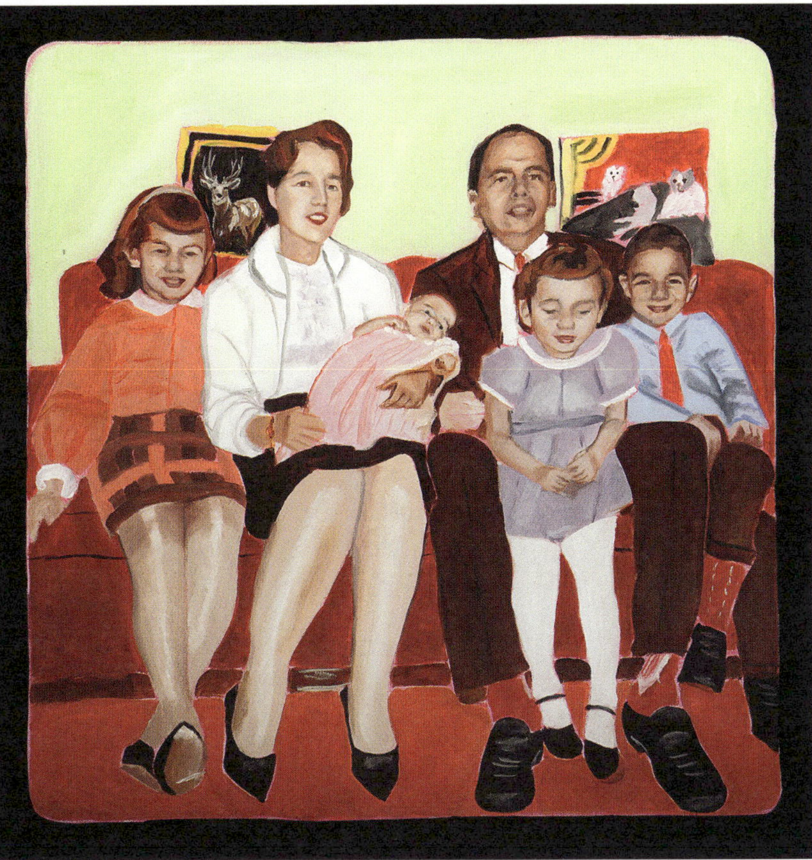

Shauntay Grant with Annie Simmonds and Shyronn Smardon

Grandmother, Teach Me is a collaborative work with my late maternal great-grandmother, Annie Simmonds, and photographer Shyronn Smardon.

My great-grandmother's handmade quilts—made from old clothing and held together by bits of yarn—move between symmetry and disproportion, pattern and free form. I'm told her hands were arthritic and her eyesight poor. She died when I was still a child, and while I have very little memory of her, I feel I have learned—and continue to learn—from her. For me, her quilts embody patience, perseverance, family, and history. I have a deep love for them, and for uncovering the stories that they keep.

Shauntay Grant Wearing Winter Quilt
by Annie Simmonds, Citadel Hill, Halifax, Nova Scotia, 2013
Digital photograph, dimensions variable
Courtesy of the artist
Photo by Shyronn Smardon

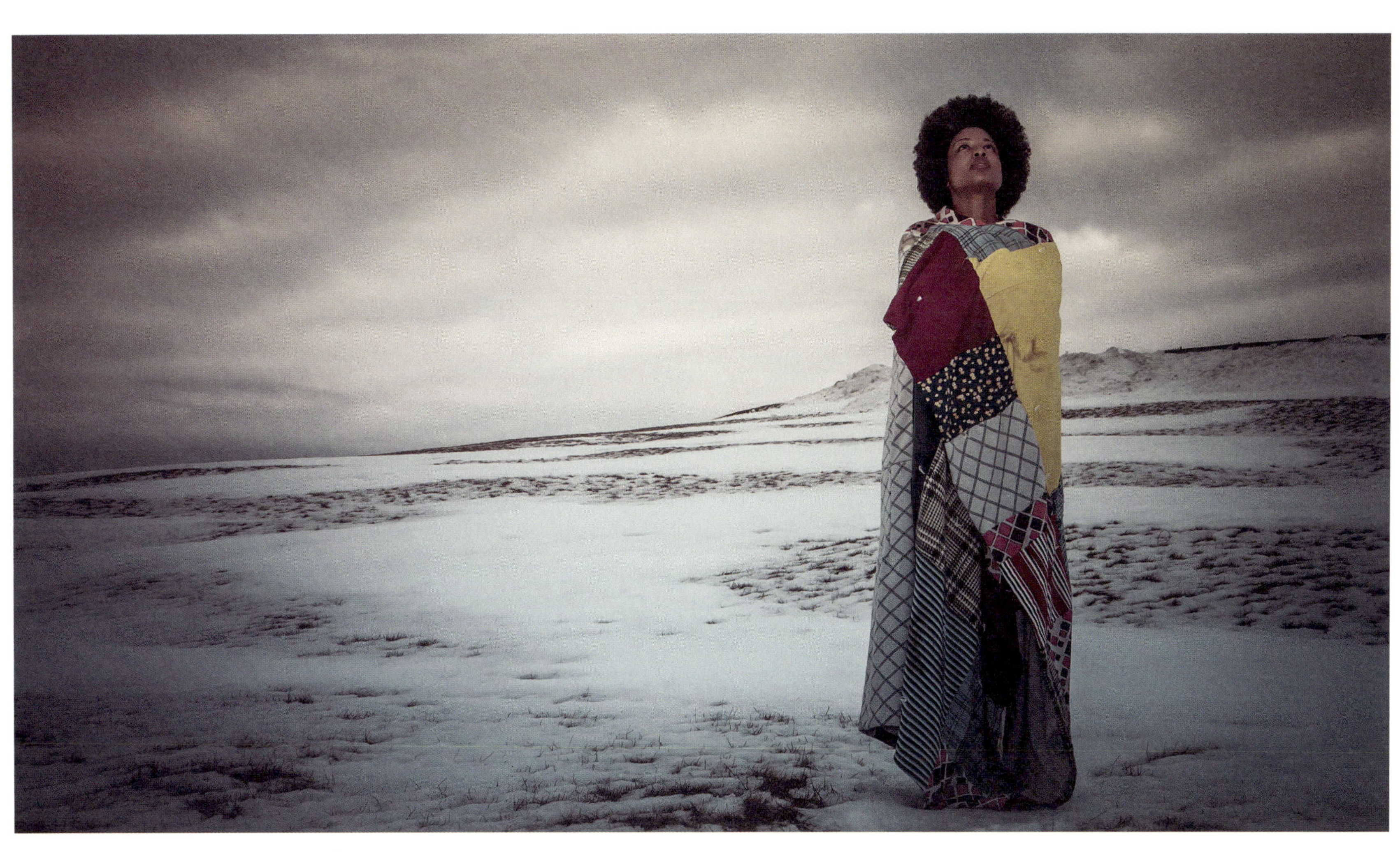

Xiong Gu

Niagara Falls is such an iconic Canadian place, but few know about the seasonal migrant workers who harvest produce in the region, or appreciate their contributions. At the busiest times of the year, these people work twelve to fourteen hour days, seven days a week. It reminds me of my time during China's Cultural Revolution when I was sent to the countryside to labour on the farms.

I think about these migrant workers' sacrifices. Many come from Jamaica and Mexico, so they leave their families for eight to ten months of the year, just to be able to earn a living and send household items to loved ones back home. The labour of migrant workers illuminates the falls—far more so than the dye used in "souvenir water," or the spotlights directed at the falls.

Illuminated Niagara Falls, 2017
Digital photographs, fruit baskets,
and souvenir water, dimensions variable
Courtesy of the artist

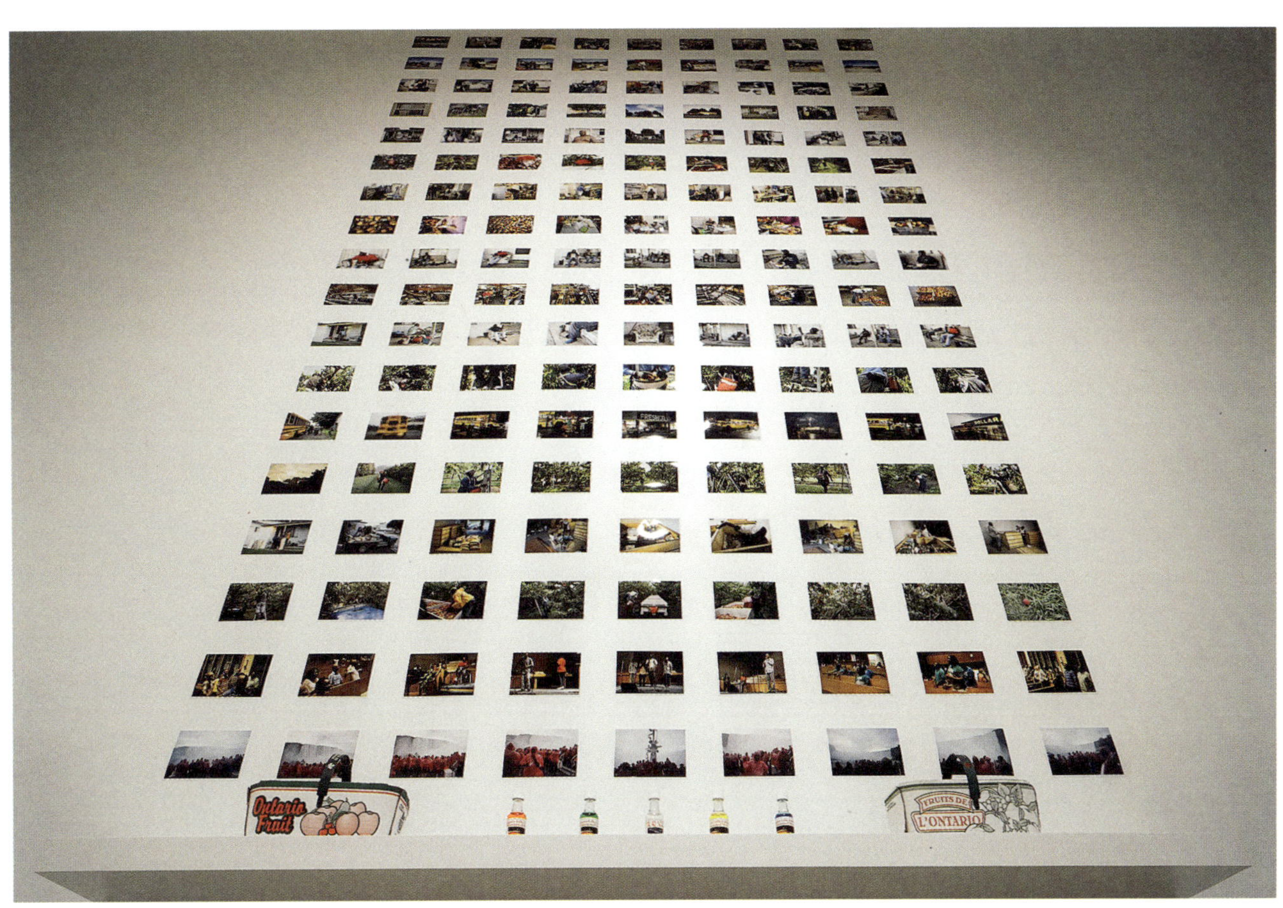
Ontario Fruit
L'ONTARIO

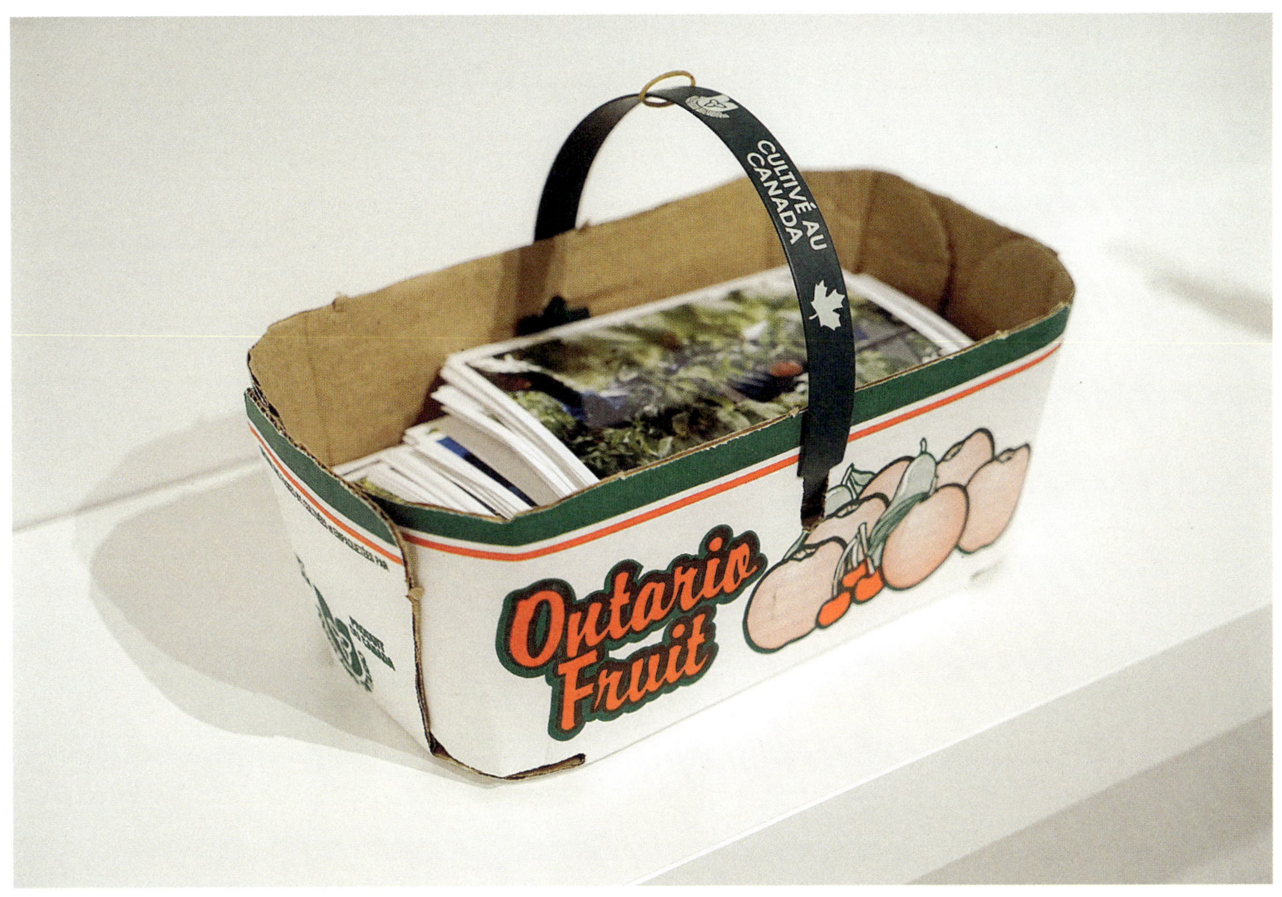
CULTIVÉ AU CANADA
Ontario Fruit

Yu Gu

These videos are about Niagara's migrant workers who spend eight to ten months of the year in Ontario, and send their wages to their families back in Jamaica or Mexico. It explores the tensions between their memories of home and their present reality.

I made this work in collaboration with my dad (artist Xiong Gu). He initiated this project from his own experience as a farmer in China when he was seventeen. He was sent to the countryside as an urban youth to be re-educated as a farmer. That was his first migration experience. His second migration was when we moved as a family from China to Vancouver.

Interior Migrations, 2017
Video stills from three-channel video installation, 12 minutes
Courtesy of the artist

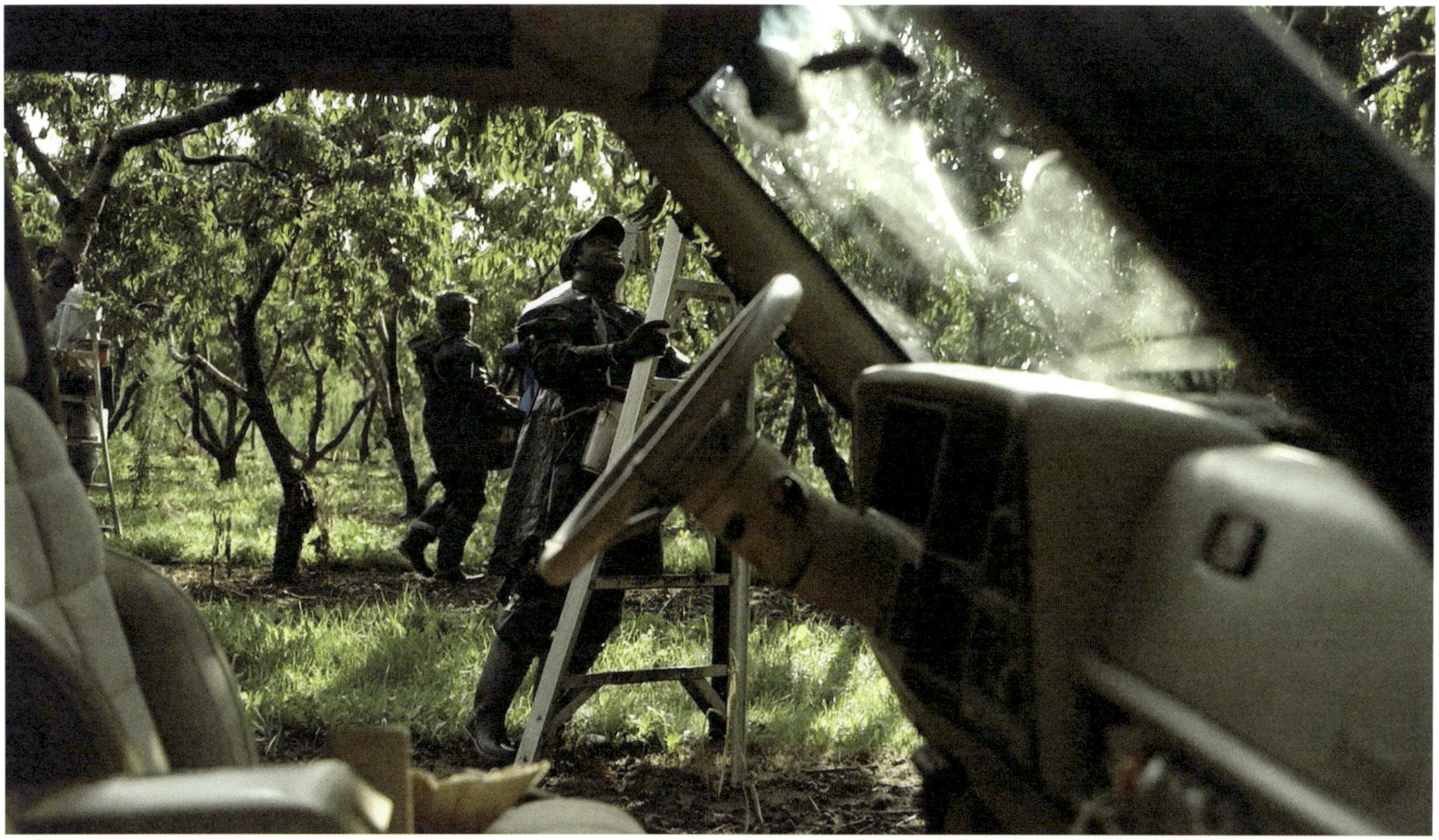

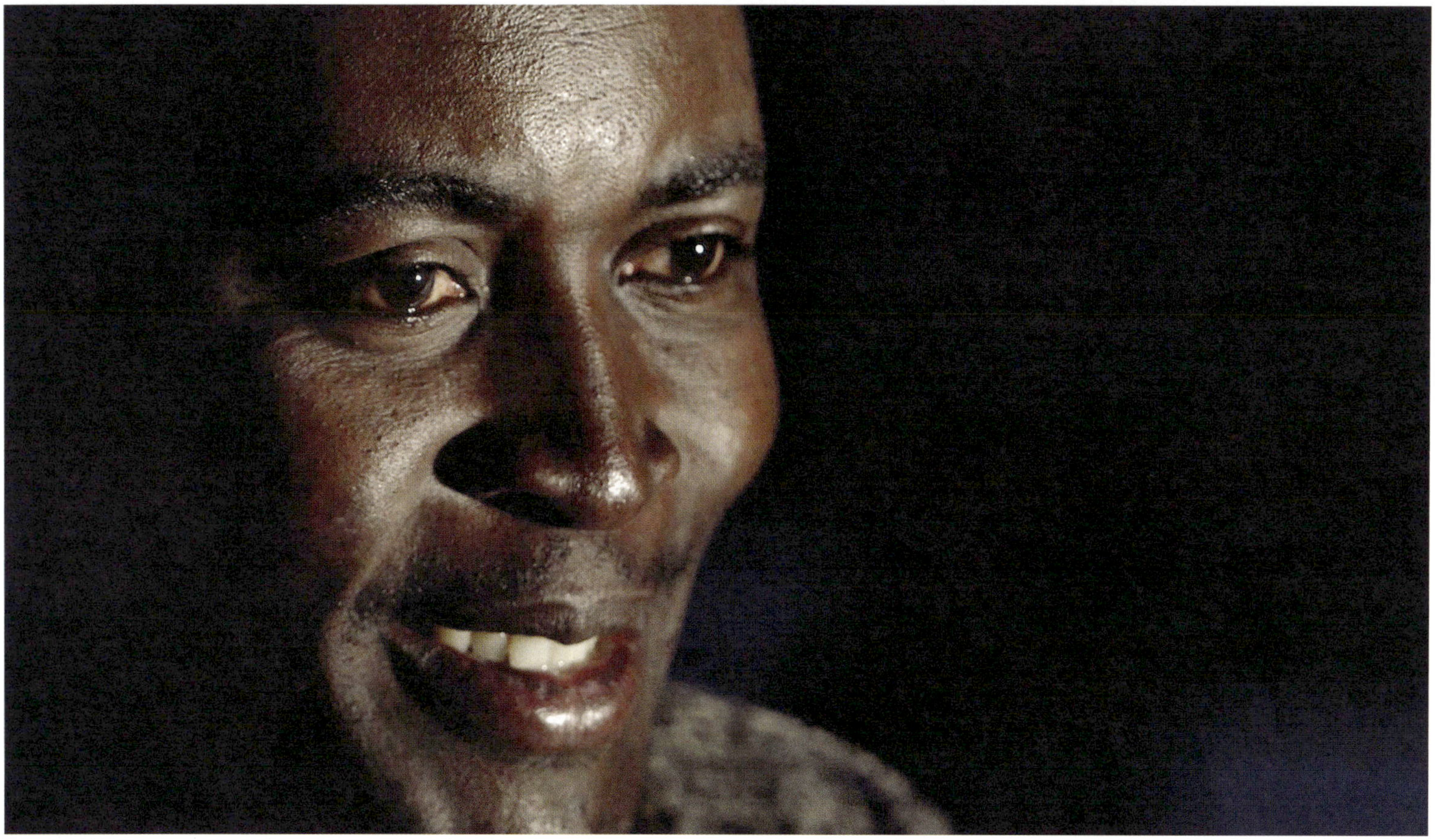

Lisa Hirmer

I was thinking about "Canadian clichés," and winter comes up a lot. It's interesting because our relationship to weather and seasonality has shifted from a common backdrop to a register of unprecedented planetary change. What does this mean for that association?

Centuries, or even just decades, into the future, winter is going to be really, really different. We may not lose snow entirely, but predictions say it will melt very quickly and we won't have the long months of heavy snow associated with "Canadian winter." The change will be gradual, so at what point can we say winter is no longer winter? When do we mourn?

Watching, dull edges, the northern hemisphere of a 23° 27' tilt, 2017
65 digital C-prints on dibond, 61 × 40.6 cm each
Courtesy of the artist

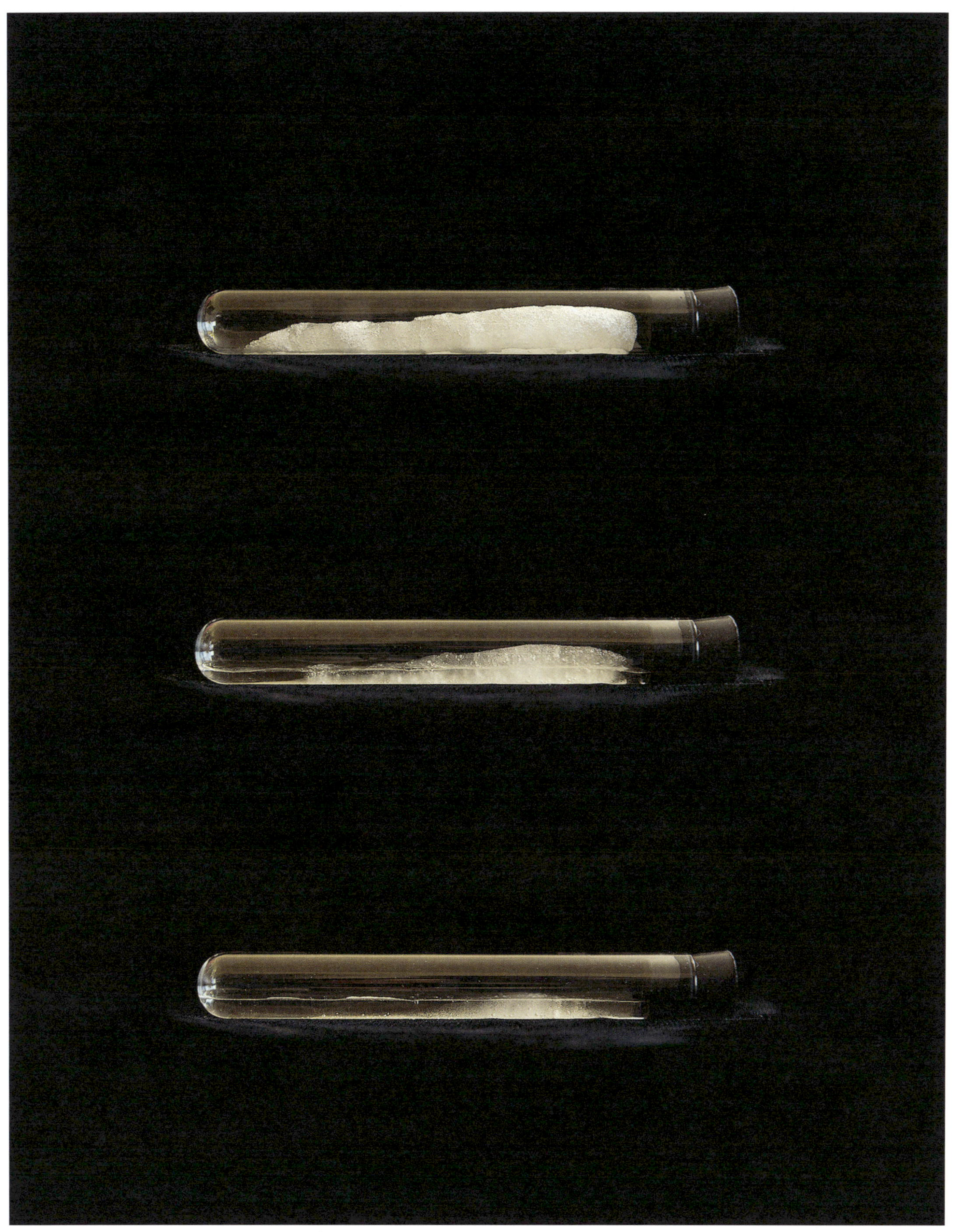

Robert Houle

This installation recreates an encounter between two groups: Mississauga leader Maungwudaus and his dance troupe, and the French royal court of 1845. Below each dancer's portrait is a painting of the smallpox virus, which killed several members of the dance troupe—of the eleven original members, only five returned.

For us, as Ojibwa people, our spirits can be locked up if we are put in a foreign place. It's an idea, but there's some truth in it. After returning to my studio in Toronto to begin the preliminary drawings for the installation, I realized that I had brought the dancers' spirits home.

Paris/Ojibwa, 2009–2010
Mixed media installation, 358 × 488 × 488 cm
Courtesy of the artist
Photo by Michael Cullen

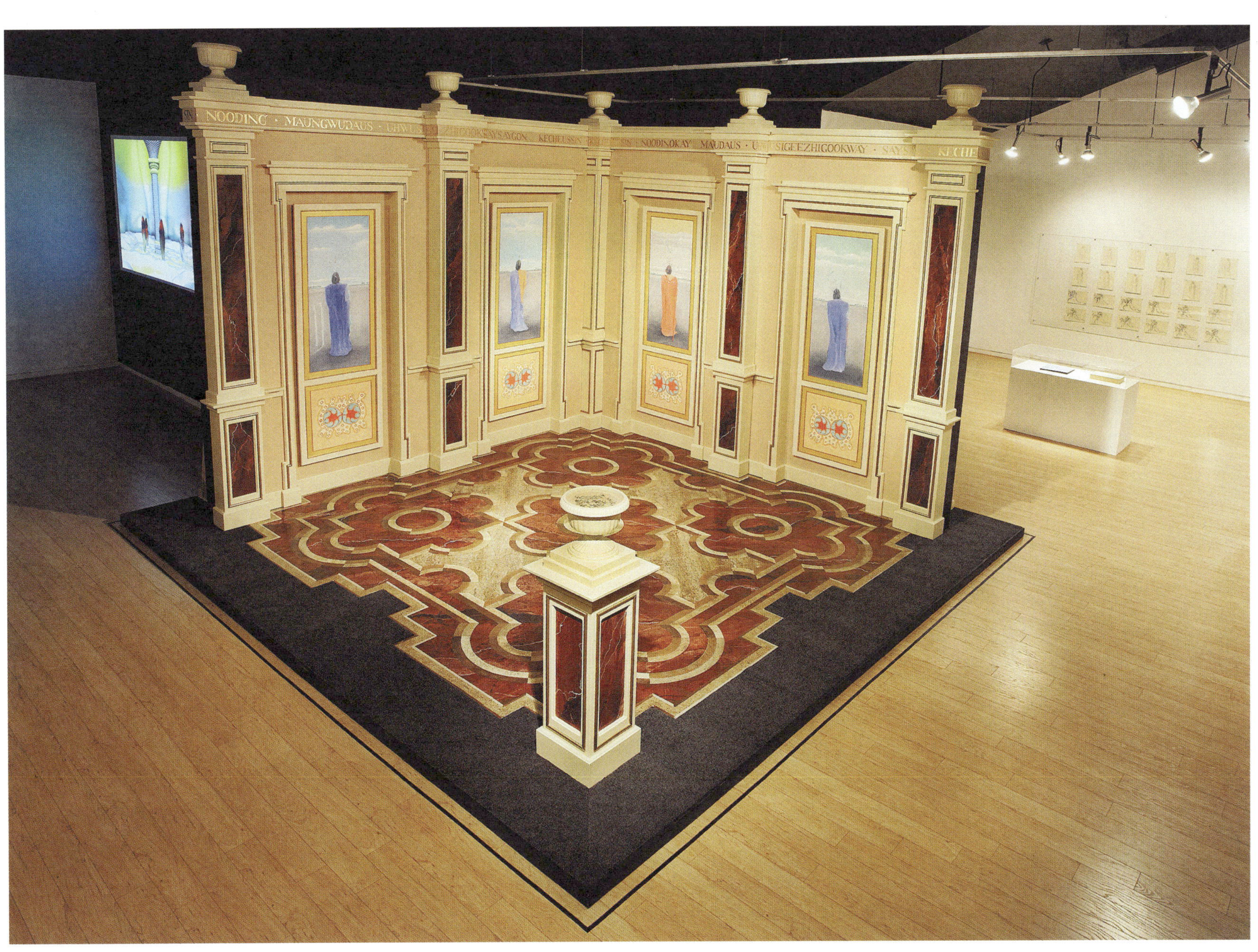
NOODING · MAUNGWUDAUS
NOODINOKAY MAUDAUS
SIGEEZHIGOOKWAY · SAYS
KECHE

Abedar Kamgari

I have been spending a lot of time thinking about my heritage and family legacy. How do I engage with these ideas as someone who has had to abandon the land of their ancestors?

This April, I left my home by the Hamilton mountain and travelled back to Iran to trace significant sites in my family's history across multiple provinces. Guided only by my relatives' nostalgic recollections and stories of places once inhabited, I had hoped to resolve my questions once and for all.

Another Country, 2017
Research image for three-channel video
Courtesy of the artist
Photo by Brian Mulhall

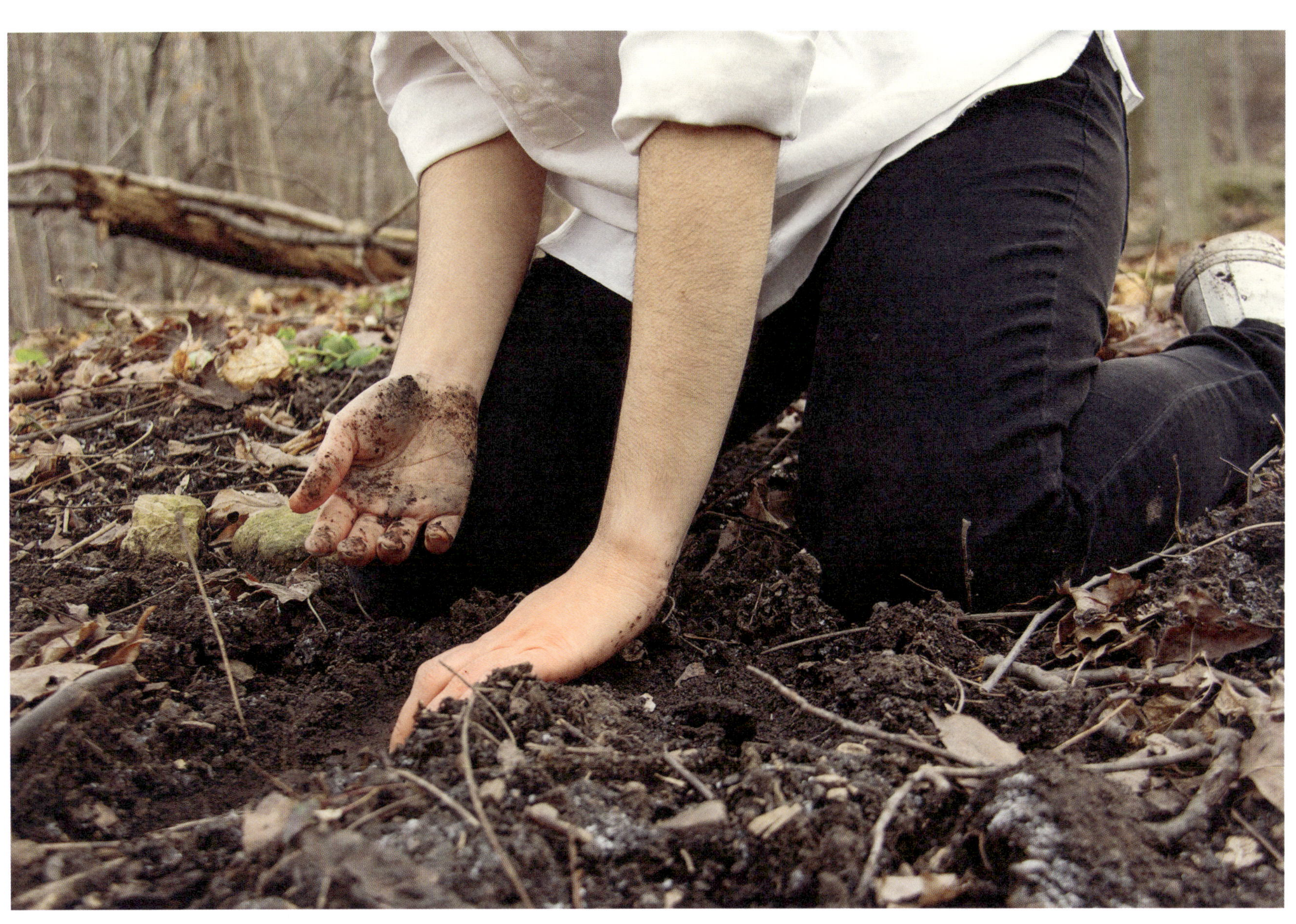

Myung-Sun Kim

elegy sculptures

your presence known in your absence
amnesia
body remembers, I do not
silenced, undocumented ~~history~~ twitching in the body
absence of memory
vessels we fill to consume you
in thoughts of you
to be momentarily immersed in the light of your presence
constant desire that will never be filled
love, even in the times of colonial past-present-future
the liquids fill the void, in shape of you
or what could be described as you
nothing resembling the way   i think of you
your constant shifting, changing body
change is inevitable
void. liquid filling into it, into me, shifting, changing me.

time being, 2016
Artist's proof, raised mud with extracted minerals and precious metal, fired up to 2269°F, 10.2 × 7.6 × 7.6 cm
Courtesy of the artist

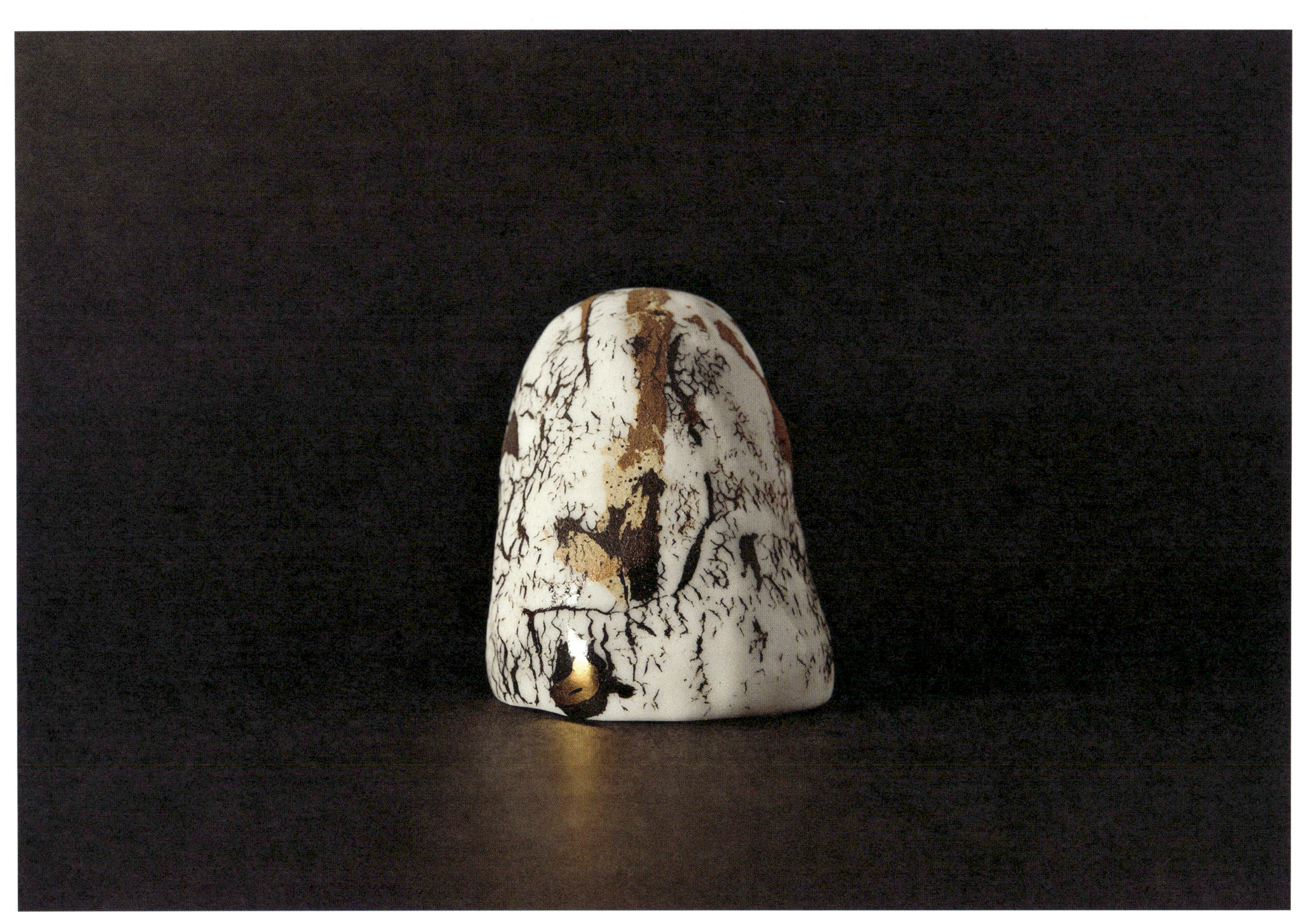

Charmaine Lurch

A Mobile and Visible Carriage retrieves written, archival, and present-day material to articulate a story that is inherently Canadian. In 1837, Thornton and Lucie Blackburn's horse-drawn cab, "The City," was the first and only cab in Upper Canada (present-day southern Ontario). It made visible the Blackburns' lived experience in Toronto, and stands as concrete evidence of people who were both activists and entrepreneurs.

The silhouetted frame of the cab and its placement on the ground incorporates memory and erasure, the visible and invisible, to locate and make tangible Black history and presence in Canada today.

A Mobile and Visible Carriage, 2015
MDF, paint, antique carriage wheel, and metal,
100 × 366 × 244 cm
Courtesy of the artist
Photo by Christina Sideris

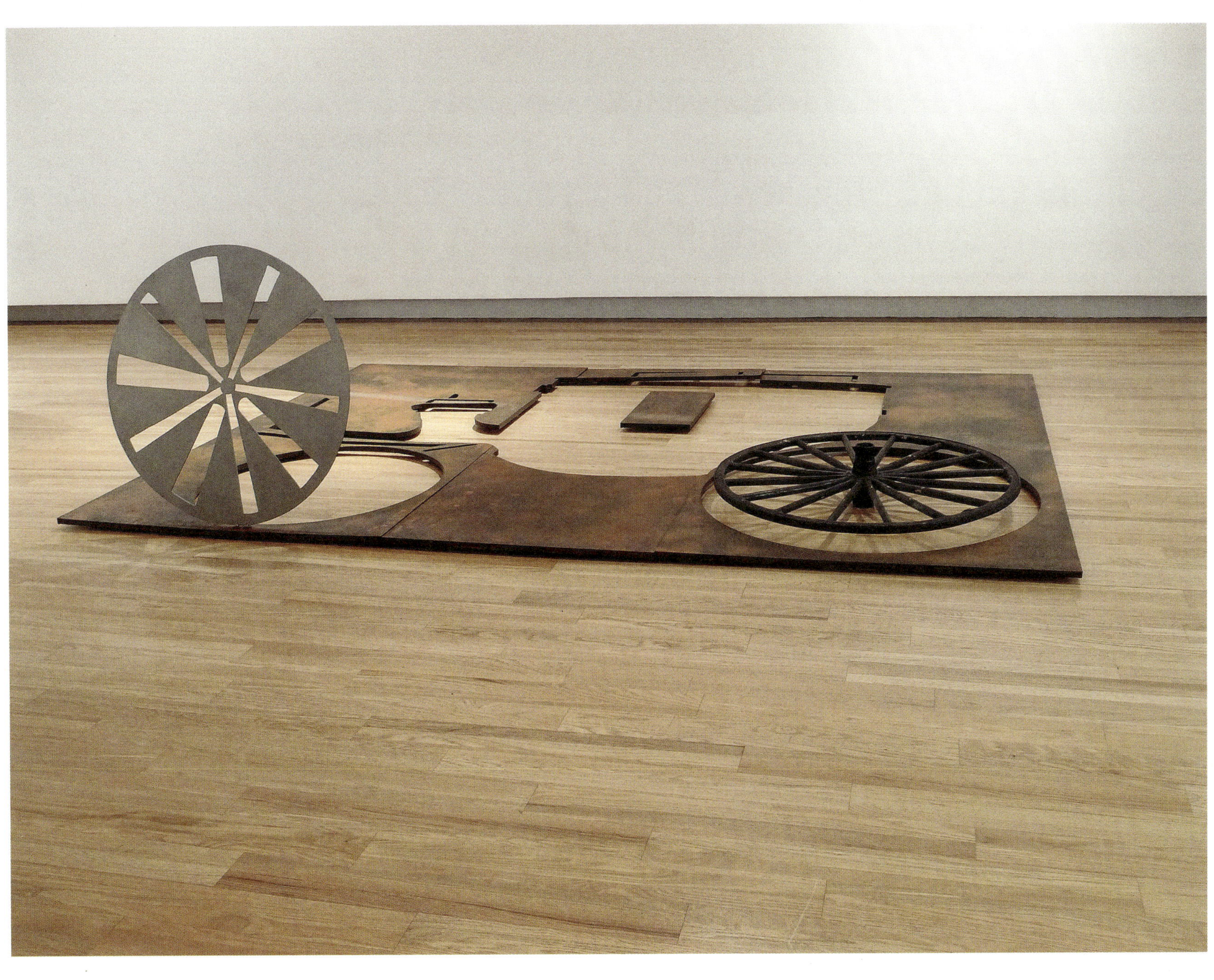

Meryl McMaster

There have been many moments in my life when the realization of how little time we have has consumed my thoughts. *Time's Gravity* reflects on these feelings of fleeting time as well as the preservation of memory. The books I am holding represent my journals throughout my life, and the drawings on the spines were inspired by "winter count" drawings used by Indigenous peoples from across North America to depict a pictorial calendar of the community's oral history. The drawings were produced as a storytelling method to mark important events from each year. I created my own winter counts to mark an important moment in my life for each year that I have been alive. I'm holding the journals in this way to hold onto these memories and not let them go. I'll always have this connection to who I am and where I'm from. That stays with me wherever I go, and informs my path in some way.

Time's Gravity, 2015
Inkjet print mounted to dibond, 76.2 × 114.3 cm
Courtesy of the artist and Katzman Contemporary

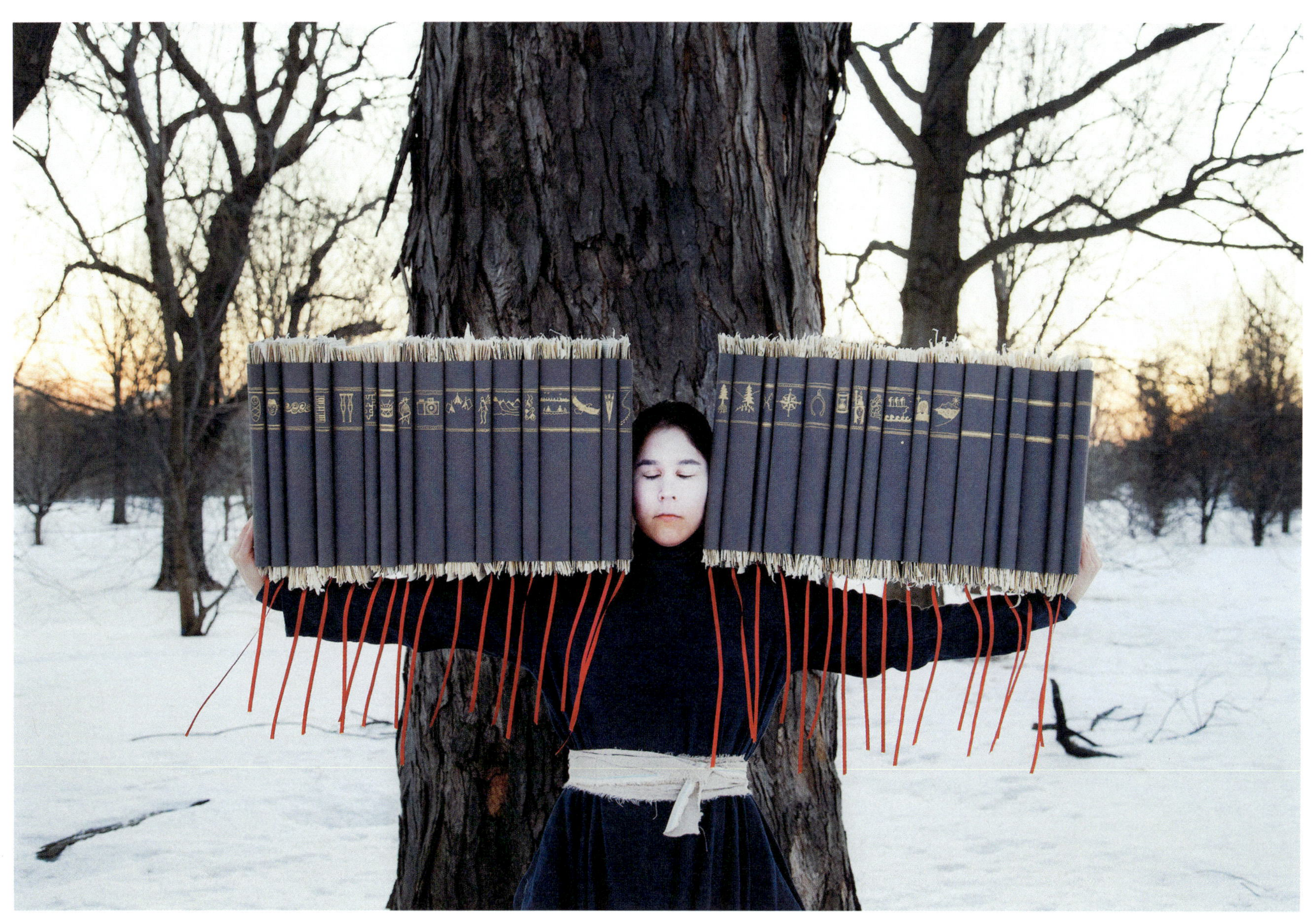

Laura Millard

Last winter I began doing large drawings on a frozen lake, using a snowmobile as the drawing tool. I've been documenting these temporary marks using a drone to photograph how the original drawings have changed and been erased by weather and over time.

These impermanent images inscribed on a place that's not mine felt like a metaphor—for land use, ownership, and the problems of Canada 150 in relation to treaty rights. This metaphor of going in circles and the absurdity of going nowhere fast was suddenly stilled by a quiet crossing.

Crossing, 2017
Water-based inks on recyclable polymer fabric and aluminum frame, 275 × 183 cm
Courtesy of the artist

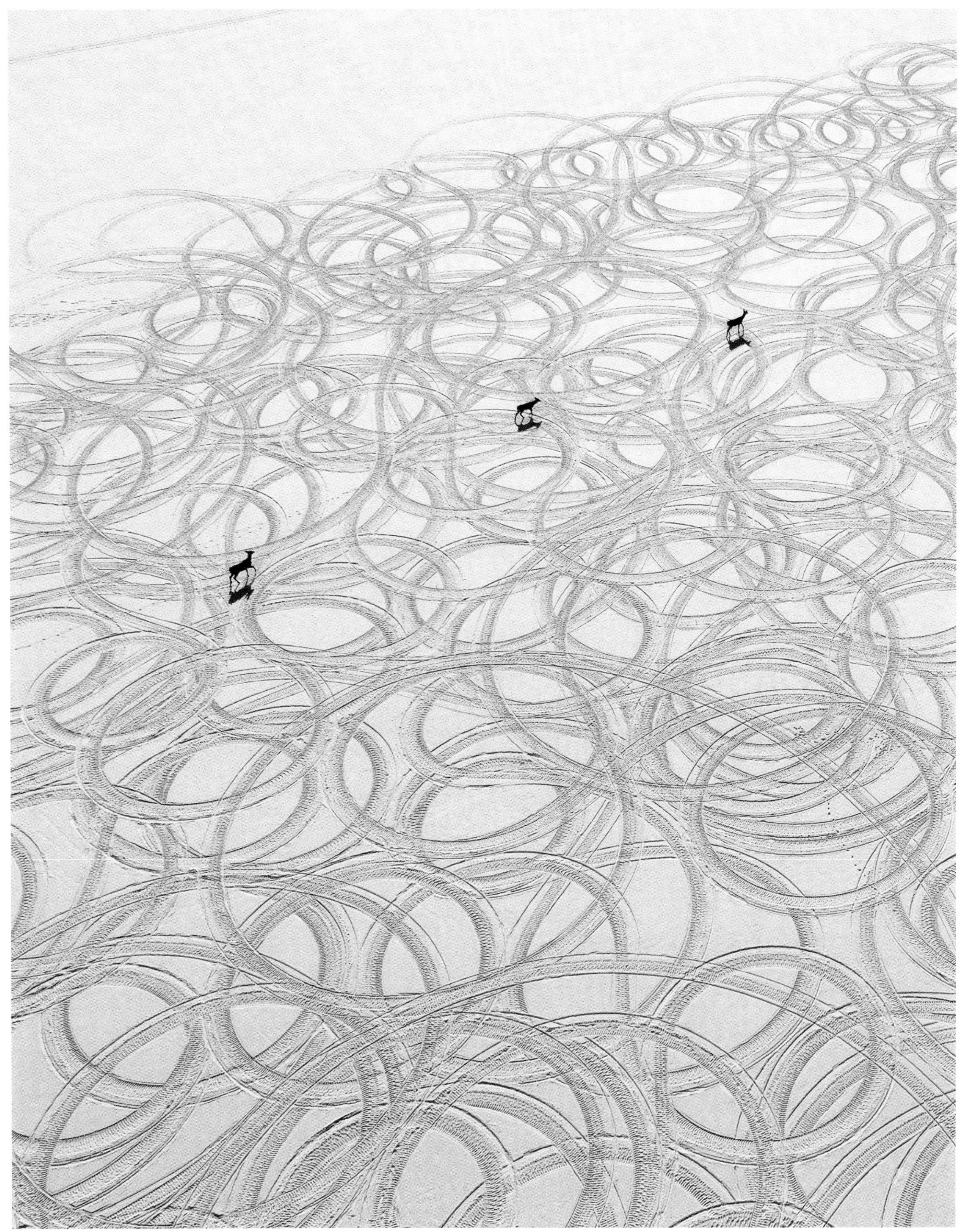

I'm exploring Black masculinity and identity in relation to society's expectations of Black men. These basketballs serve as a metaphor for the deflated hoop dreams of Black men in North America.

Only thirty men enter the NBA every year. I often think about all the Black men across North America who grow up thinking they're going to get into the NBA. They rely on the fact that they're going to become wealthy basketball players, and when they don't make it into the NBA, they have nothing to fall back on. This felt so heavy to me. The concrete basketballs are physically heavy but also so fragile—the nature of concrete is to crack, so eventually these will break apart.

Heavy, Heavy (Hoop Dreams), 2016
Concrete on black Plexiglas, 3 × 3 m
Courtesy of the artist

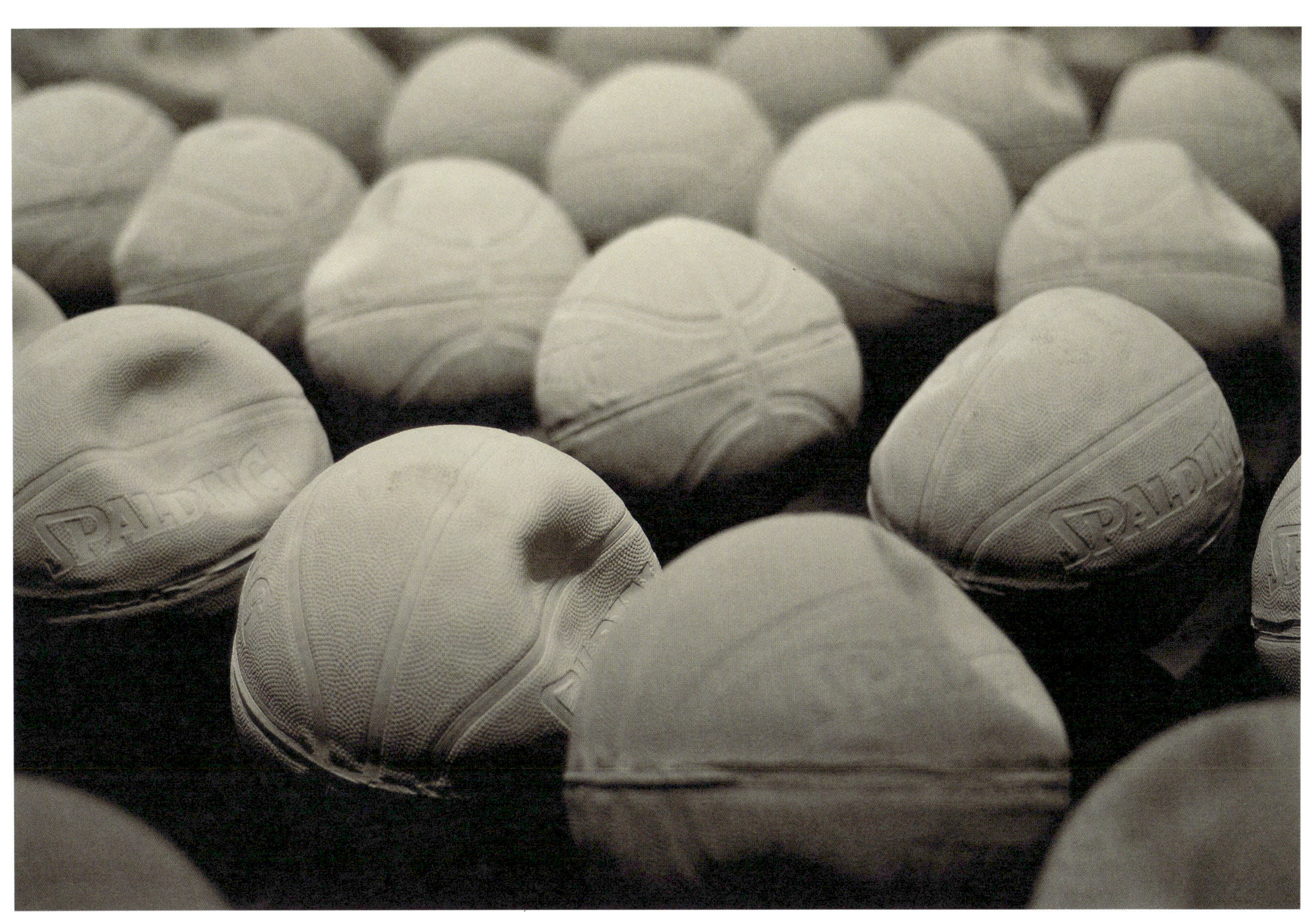

Norval Morrisseau

Why am I alive? To heal you guys who are more screwed up than I am. How can I heal you? With colour. These are the colours you dreamt about one night. I paint with these colours to heal; my paintings honour the Anishinaabe ancestors who have roamed the Great Lakes for centuries upon centuries.

Untitled (Misshipeshu the Water God, Water Beings, and Earth Mother), around 1965
Acrylic, oil, and ink over graphite on paper, 81.2 × 198.1 cm
Private collection
Photo by the Art Gallery of Ontario

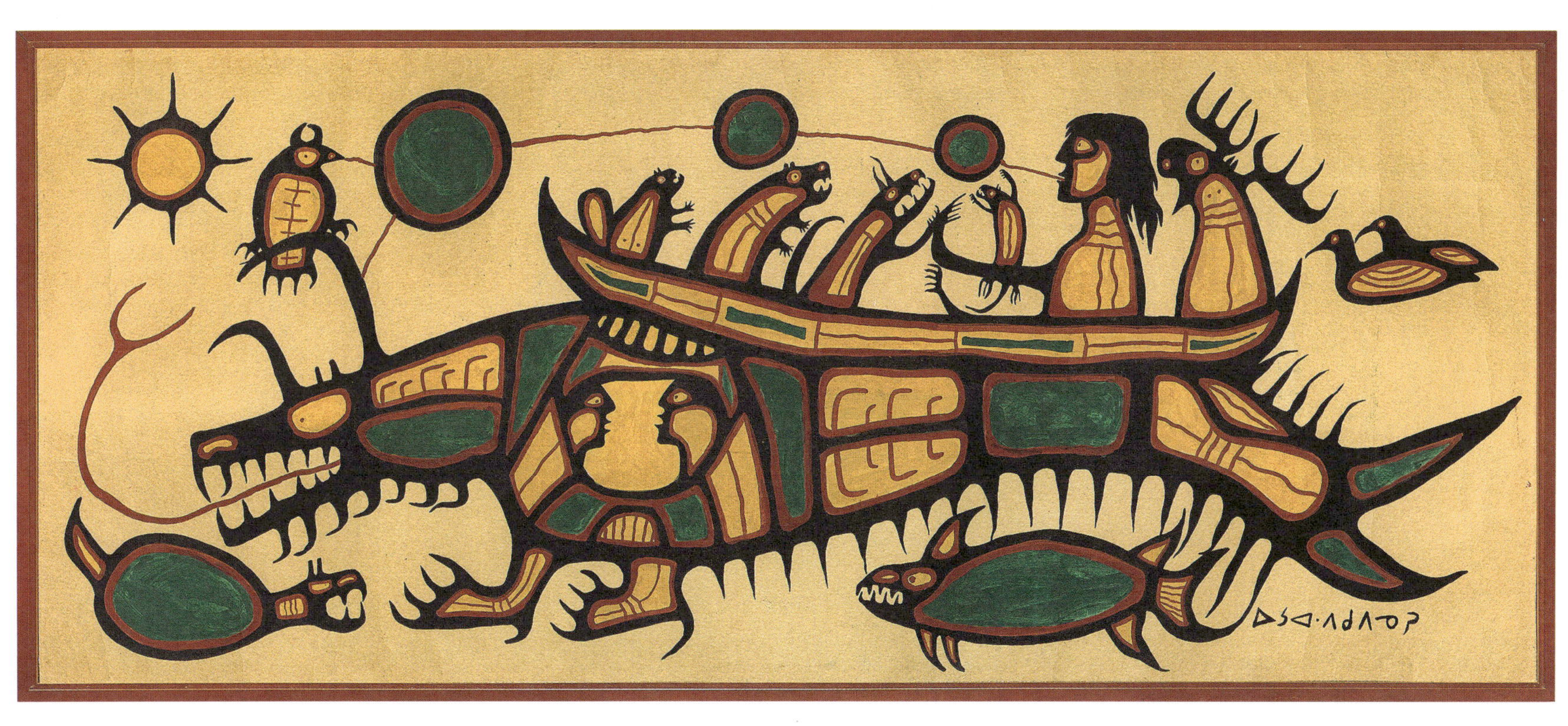
ᐅᓴᐘᐱᑯᐱᓀᓯ

Lisa Myers

The animation of berries morphs between changing landforms and waterways into impressions of mass inhabitation of places and spaces—in all, the berries end up as the beings that exist underground and underwater, leaving a reddish swath. I created this animation in response to a walk I took in the summer of 2009, following the route described by my grandfather as he fled from residential school by walking eastward from Sault Ste. Marie along the train tracks.

and from then on we lived on blueberries for about a week, 2013
Video still from digital video, 45 seconds, looped
Courtesy of the artist

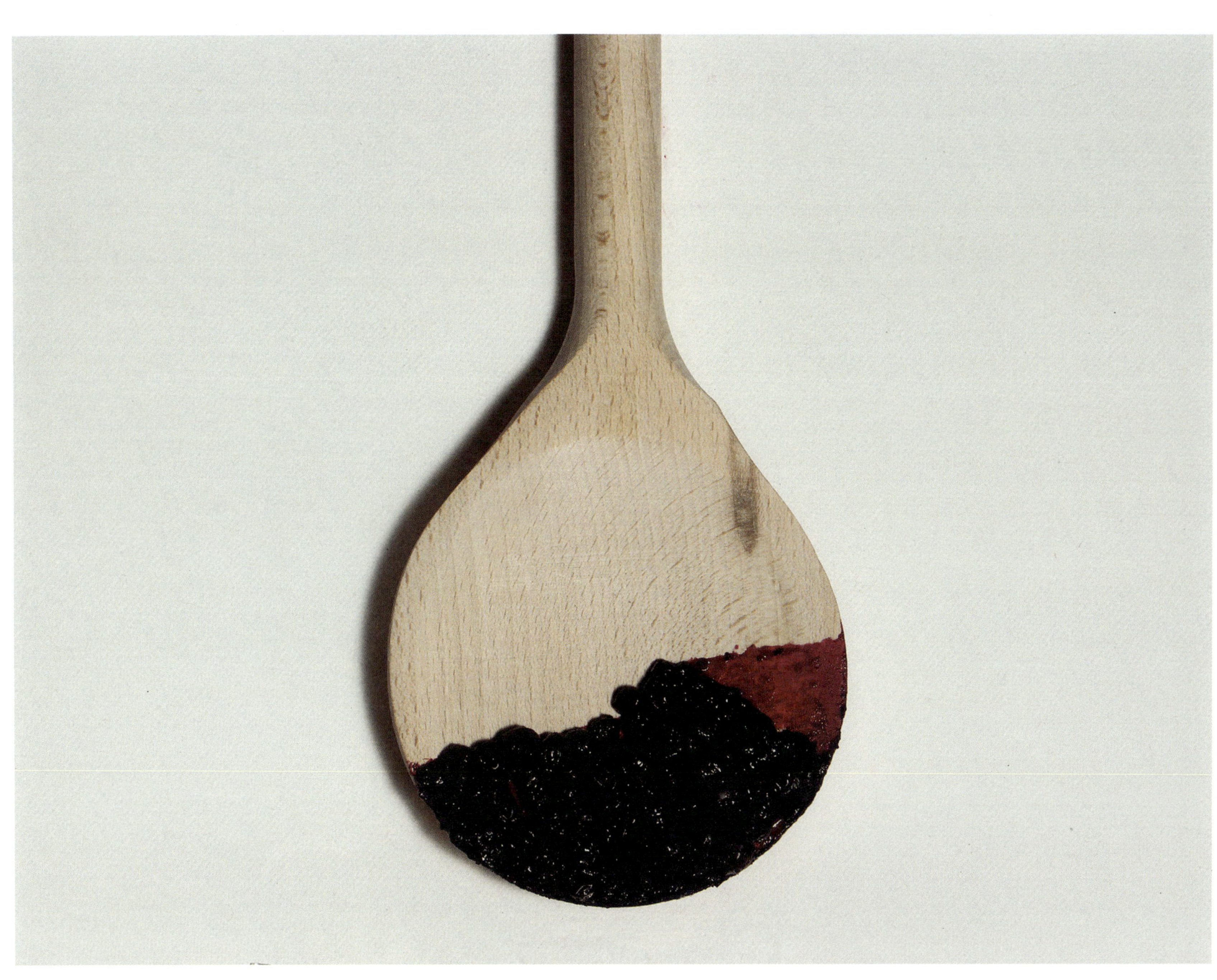

We're trying our best to support kids getting onto the land. Going on the land with Inuit elders transmits traditional knowledge. Every kid deserves to access their culture. Beyond cultural persistence, going on the land contributes to wellness, food security, and inspiration for artwork.

—Alexa Hatanaka and Patrick Thompson, PA System

Embassy of Imagination is a multidisciplinary arts initiative for youth based in Kinngait, Nunavut, led by artists Alexa Hatanaka and Patrick Thompson (PA System).

Towards Something New and Beautiful + Future Snowmachines in Kinngait, 2017
Process image, play-dough sculptures by Christine Adamie, Nathan Adla, Koonoo Akesuk, Latch Akesuk, Janice Allooloo, Moe Kelly, Saaki Nuna, Taqialuk Nuna, David Pudlat, Tommy Quvianaqtuliaq, Janice Qimirpik, and Cie Taqiasuk
Courtesy of the artists and Giles Spence Morrow

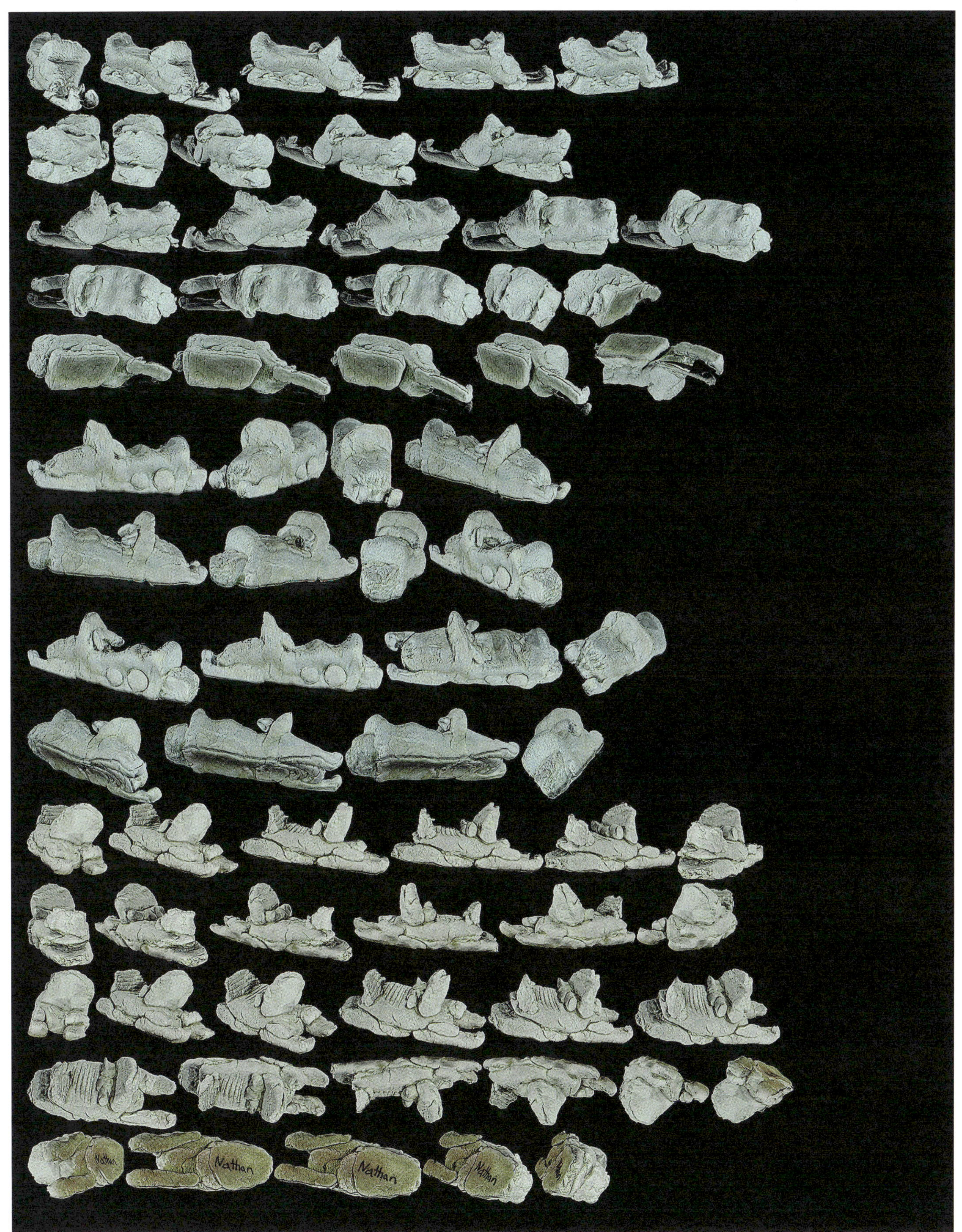
Nathan
Nathan
Nathan
Nathan

Sea Change is a collaboration with Merrell-Ann S. Phare. We're fortunate to have an abundance of fresh water in Canada, but about two-thirds of First Nations communities have had or continue to have unsafe water due to waterborne diseases and other harmful pollutants.

The texts in *Sea Change* are from Merrell-Ann's book *Denying the Source: The Crisis of First Nations Water Rights*. She's rewritten them in future-perfect tense so we can contemplate why these aren't yet true.

Sea Change, 2017
3M reflective film and gems, 320 × 508 cm
Courtesy of the artists
Photo by Ed Pien

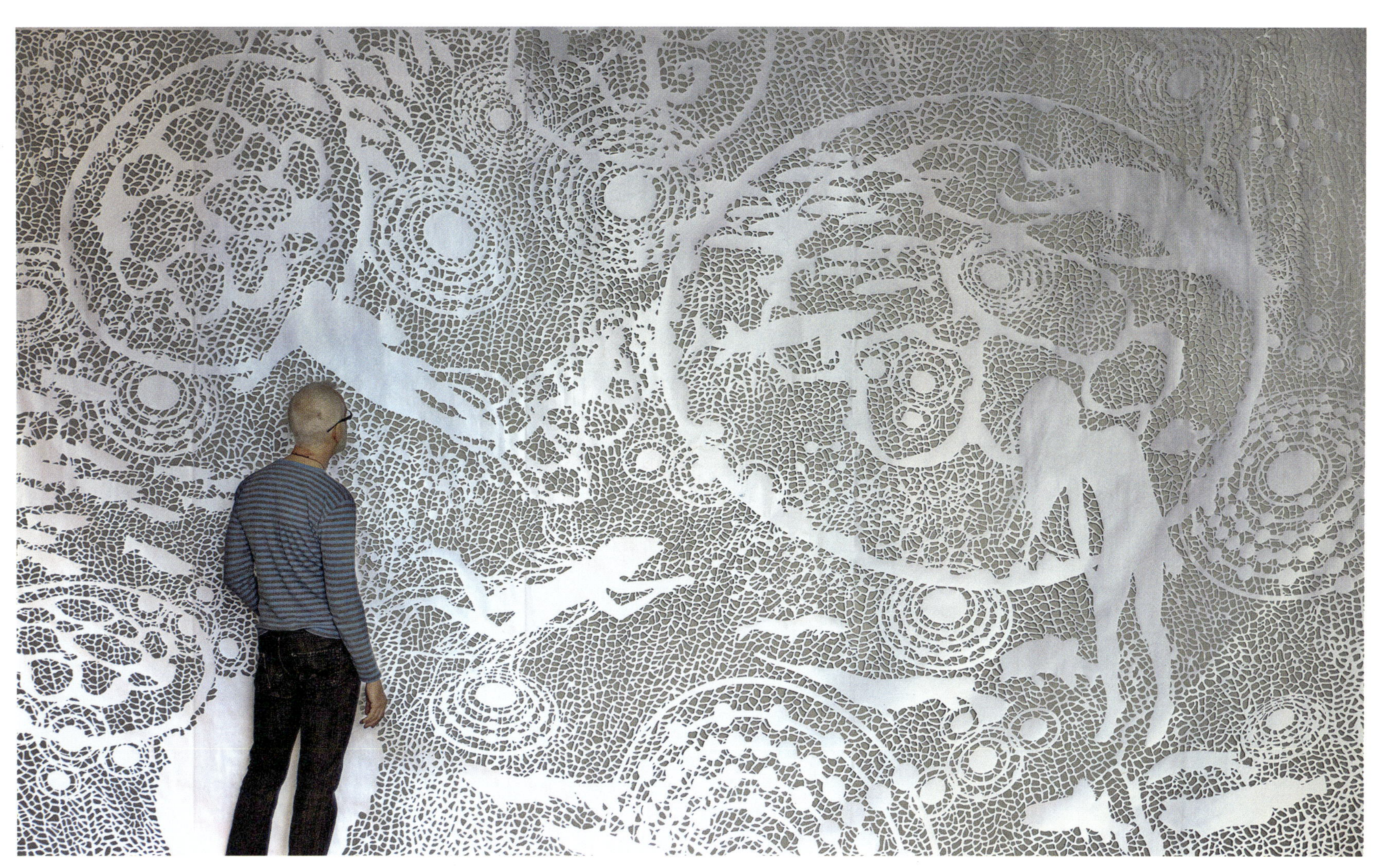

Camal Pirbhai and Camille Turner

These images are inspired by actual ads Canadian slave owners placed in newspapers about enslaved people who had escaped. We wanted to restore their humanity by viewing them as people performing freedom.

They're a part of Canadian history but not really within our education system—it feels like we're missing pieces of that past. The work we've been doing is to just understand what happened, what it means, and how has this past shaped the moment we're living in.

Bell (Wanted Series), 2016–2017
Digital photograph, dimensions variable
Courtesy of the artists, with many thanks to
Andrew Hunter, Anique Jordan and AGO staff
Photo by Christina Sideris

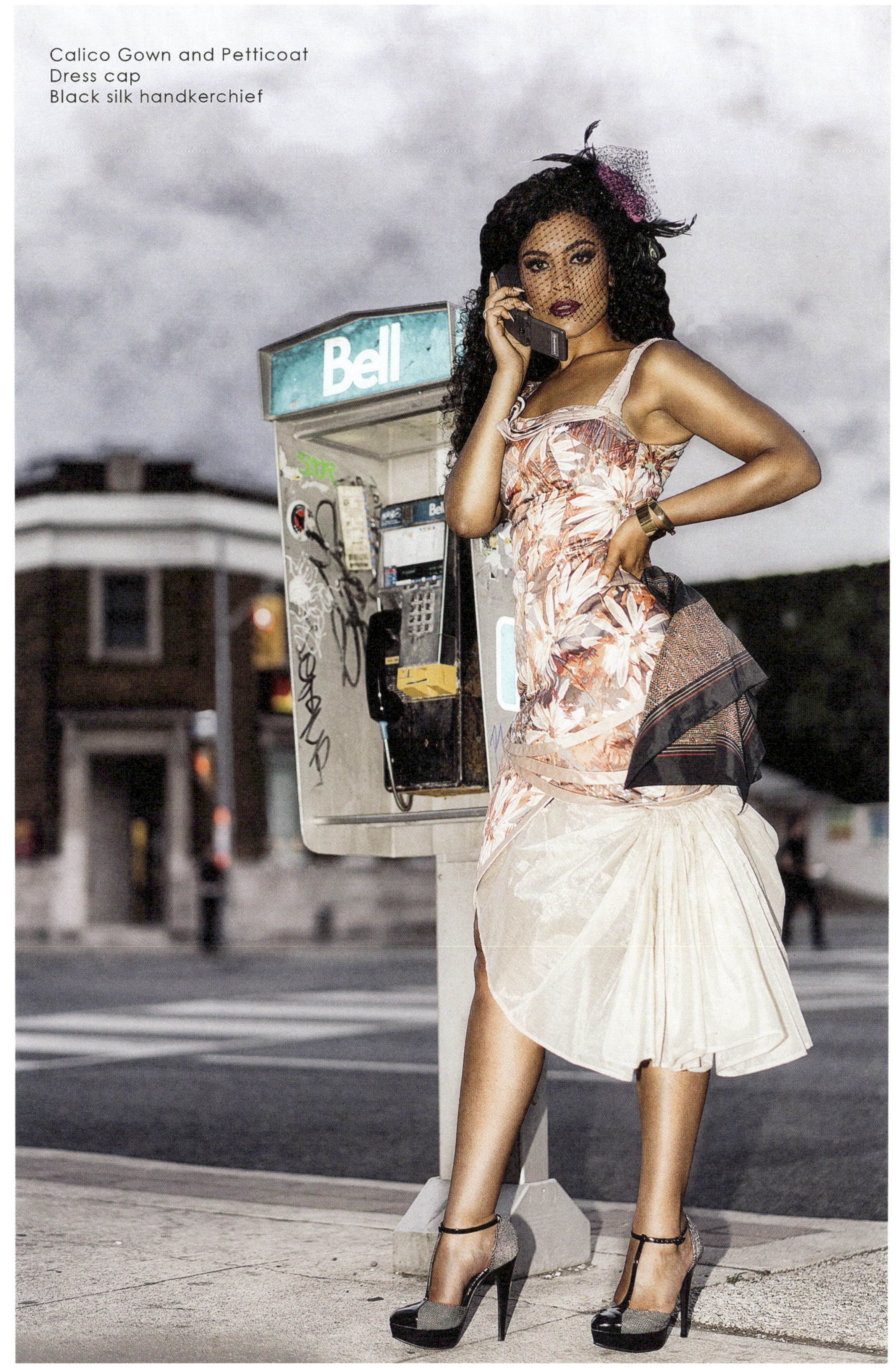

Calico Gown and Petticoat
Dress cap
Black silk handkerchief

Tim Pitsiulak

I am a hunter and I know the land and animals of the North. I have also drawn the things I see around me in the community, like boats, heavy equipment and airplanes. My inspiration to be an artist comes from my aunt, Kenojuak Ashevak, because she is the oldest and the best.

EET-EEPOW the Legend, 2014
Coloured pencil and graphite on paper, 76.2 × 111.8 cm
Collection of the Art Gallery of Ontario

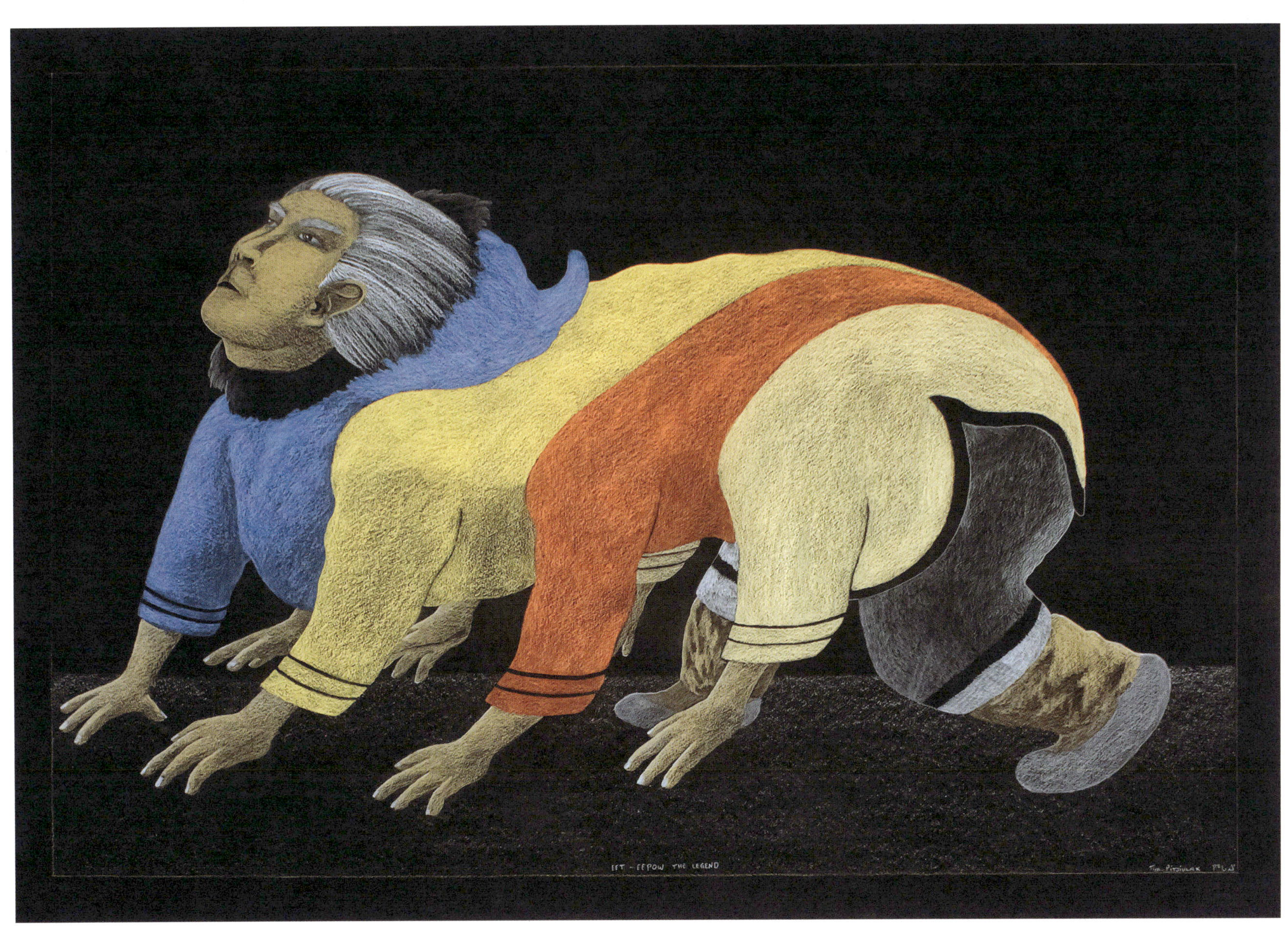
EET - EEPOW THE LEGEND
TIM PITSIULAK

Curtis Talwst Santiago

I'm beginning to notice a theme in my work. In the last couple of years I have been interested in unpacking the stories and experiences I have around race. And not just my own. My time with Lawrence Paul Yuxweluptun made me aware of the struggles of his people, which then made me cast my gaze even further to look at other minimized voices.

Here (Gaia's Door) I, 2015
Mixed media in reclaimed jewelry box,
3.8 × 3.8 × 3.8 cm

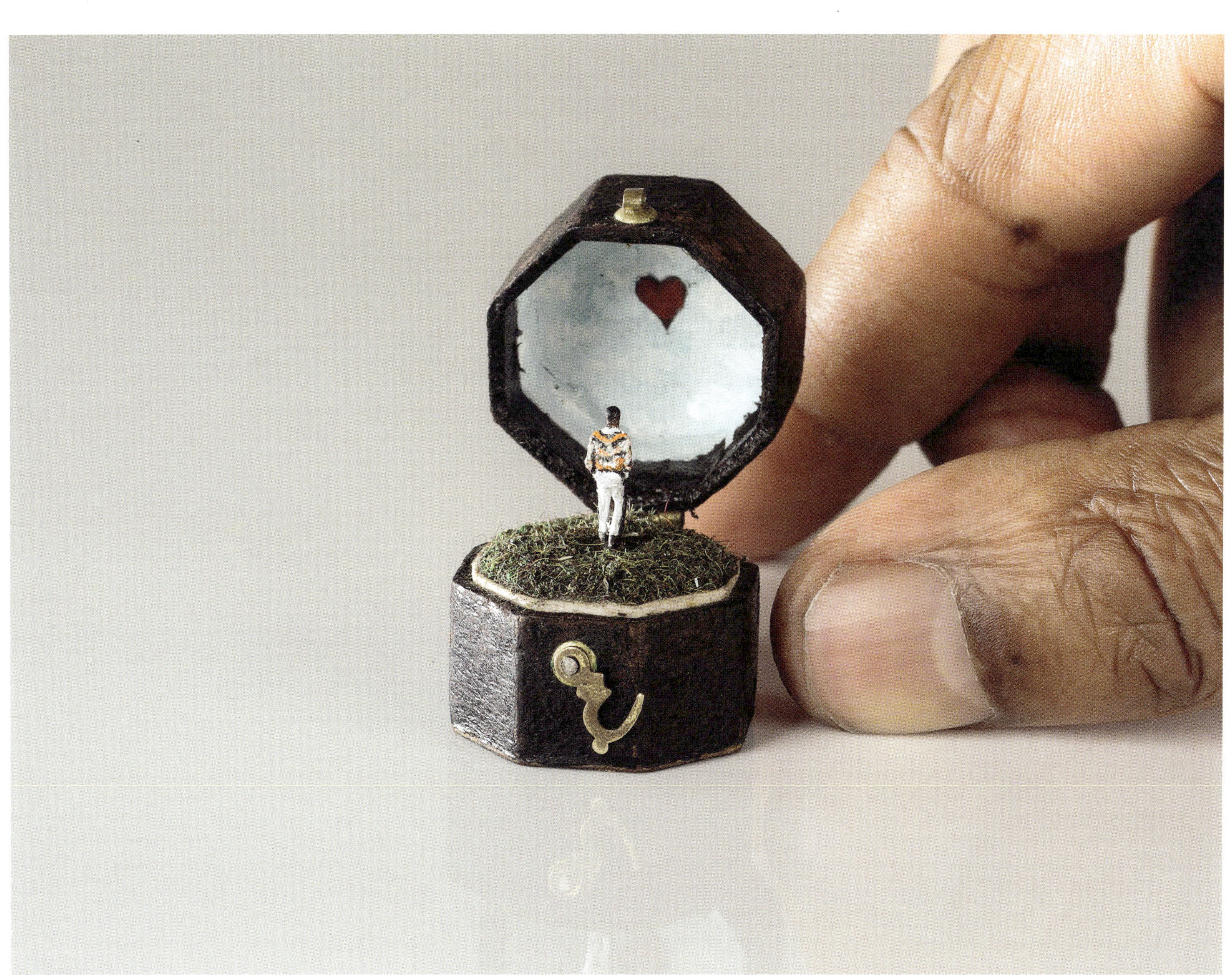

Seth

Dominion began as a "world-building" exercise connected to a graphic novel I was planning. I needed to invent the history of an imaginary city, and the models were part of that process. Eventually, the model city became more interesting to me than the graphic novel.

These buildings are made of common household materials, and are a little frayed around the edges. I hope this transmits the shopworn feeling of twentieth-century Ontario. I feel a deep connection to that mid-century landscape. *Dominion* has nothing to do with longing for a golden age. It is more about a very familiar time and place, and the melancholic pleasure the grouping of such shapes evokes.

Dominion, 2001–ongoing
Acrylic on cardboard and mixed media,
100 buildings, variable installation
Courtesy of the artist

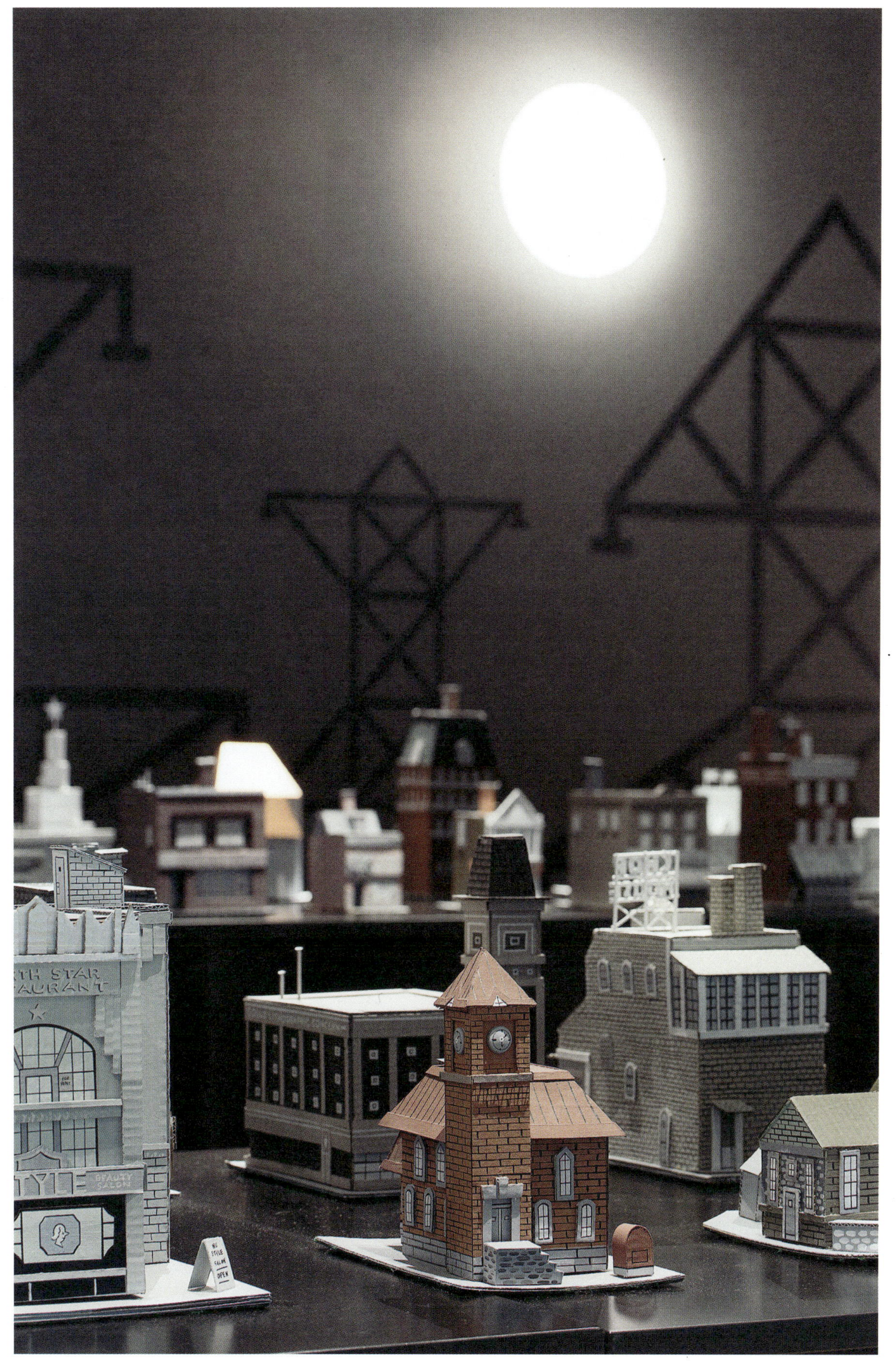
BEAUTY
SALON
OPEN

The memory of Canada's role during the war in Vietnam is one of neutrality and sanctuary for Americans resisting the draft. But at the same time, our government was selling weapons and supplies for the US war machine—including napalm—and testing Agent Orange on our own soil.

In this work, we are exploring this moral contradiction—how Canada welcomed draft dodgers but still reaped enormous profits from the war. Of course, this story is about fifty years old. Today the question is: What contemporary contradictions are Canadians living with right now?

The afternoon knows what the morning never suspected (*Swedish proverb)*, 2017
Video still from 3-channel video with sound, dimensions variable
Courtesy of the artists

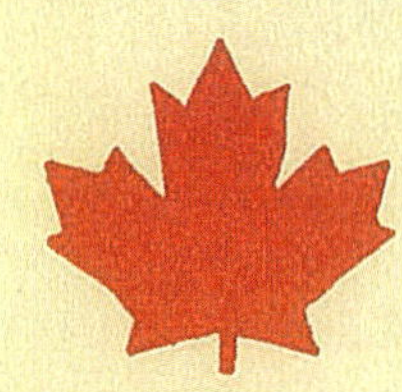

Manual
For Draft-Age Immigrants
To Canada

nineteen
sixty-eight

twenty
eighteen

This project, with artist and curator Greg Hill, began with the alteration of a prominent public monument—the Samuel de Champlain monument in Ottawa, made in 1918. It had a kneeling Anishinaabe scout at the base that was originally supposed to be paddling a canoe, but the artist couldn't complete it because the money that was needed wasn't raised. So for all these decades the scout looked submissive, kneeling at Champlain's feet.

In 1999, the kneeling figure was removed and placed across the street. I invited Greg to bring his canoe up on the platform, to see what the monument may have looked like fully finished.

Seize the Space, 2000
Digital photograph, dimensions variable
Courtesy of the artist

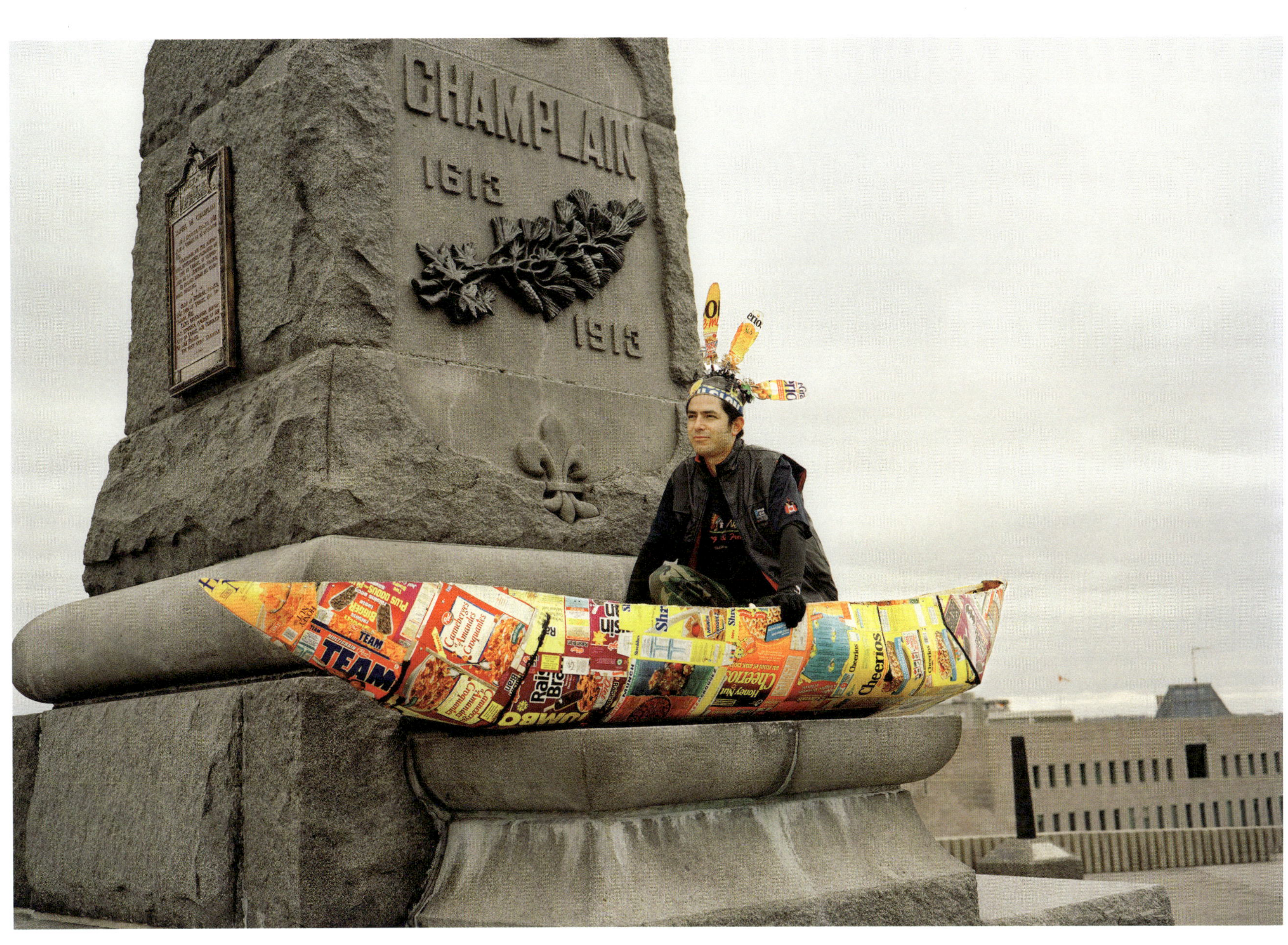
CHAMPLAIN
1613
1913
TEAM
Cheerios

These are portraits of local activists in the movement for Black lives. One of the images is of activist Yusra Khogali, who's a Black Muslim organizer with Black Lives Matter – Toronto. Yusra's been unfairly criticized for her valid comments about white supremacy in Canada.

I want to celebrate Yusra's bravery and energy, because it's easy to attack someone who seems like a representative of something, and forget they're an actual human being with feelings, families, and communities. To me, people like Yusra—and activists Melisse Watson, Dainty Smith, Kyisha Williams, and Ravyn Wngz—are essential, because we need them in the fight. They're my people and I need them to survive. That's why I'm drawing them.

Baby, Don't Worry, You Know That We Got You, 2017
Graphite on paper, 610 × 365 cm
Courtesy of the artist
Photo by the Art Gallery of Ontario

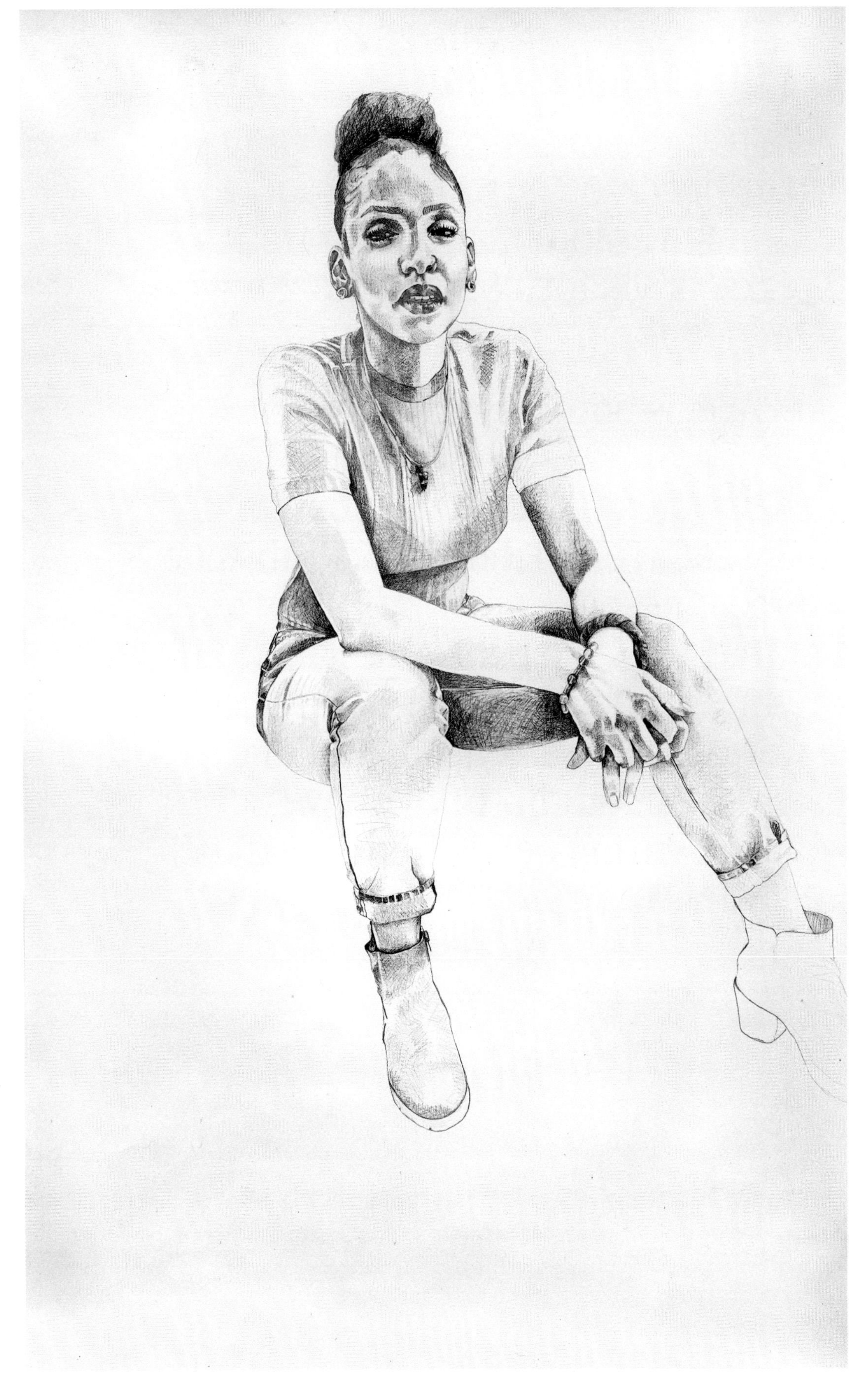

Tyshan Wright

The abeng and the drums—the bass, the rackla, and the gumbe—are the Maroons' most sacred instruments. We celebrate and communicate with our ancestors through them.

The work I share here is both past and present. When Jamaican Maroons were exiled to Nova Scotia in 1796, they were denied their ceremonial instruments. So I want to bring these sacred objects to this land and reconnect Maroon traditions to the Canadian narrative. Using natural products and fabric from three countries, I share work that represents the water crossings that are part of the Maroon story—from our origins in Ghana to the Trelawny Town Maroons' exile from Jamaica to Nova Scotia.

Gumbe I, 2017
Wood, Kente cloth, goat skin, and natural beads, 52.7 × 34.9 cm
Courtesy of the artist
Photo by Steve Farmer

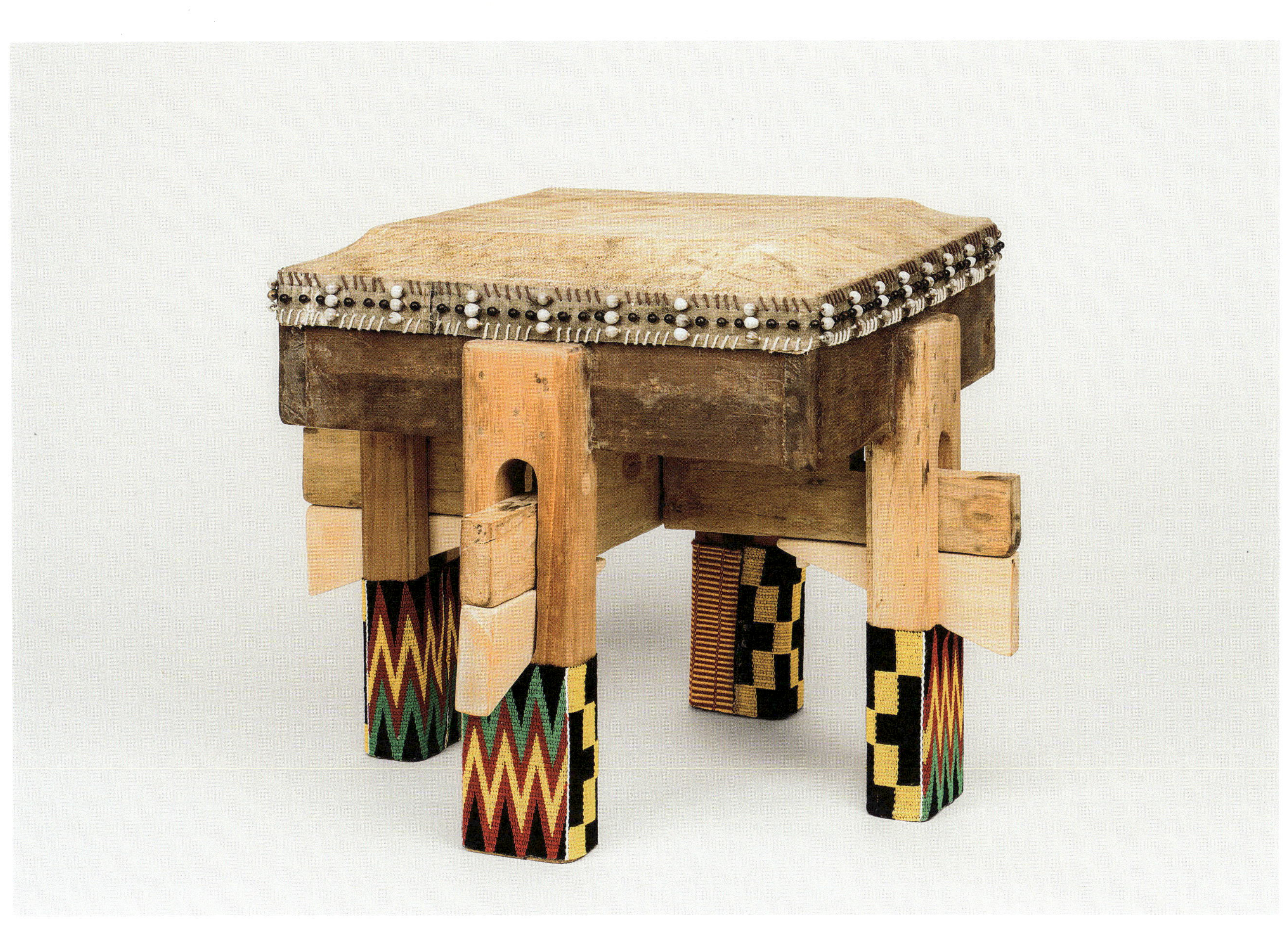

Lawrence Paul Yuxweluptun

I am a survivor, and I will freely emancipate myself as a thinking person, and I will walk in my traditional territory, and I will talk to this world; and some time, at some point, things will change.

Multi-National Conglomerates Hostile Take Over of the New World Order, 2017
Acrylic on canvas, 305 × 335 cm
Courtesy of the artist and Macaulay & Co. Fine Art
Photo by Rachel Topham

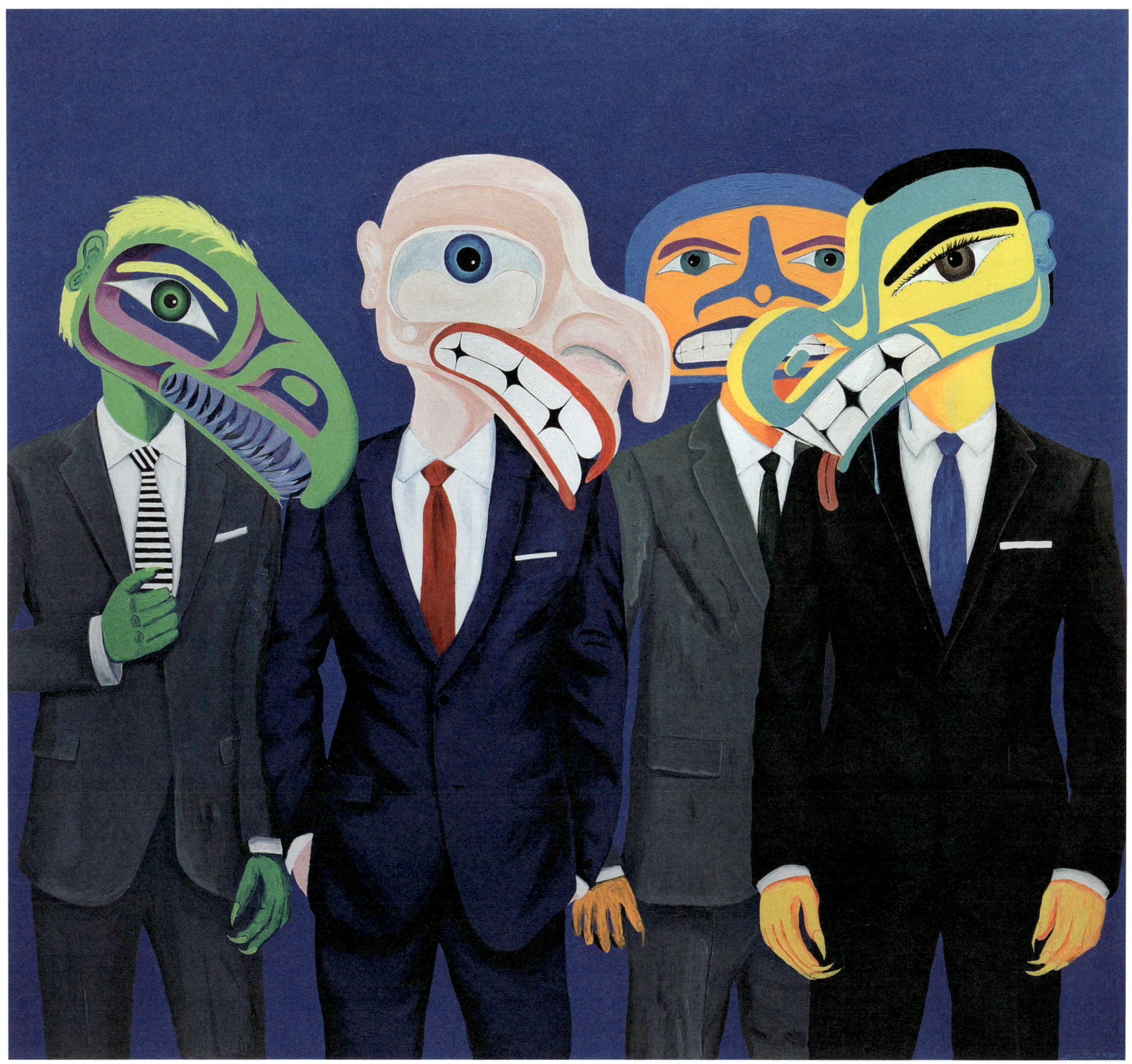

An exhibition within an exhibition, this group of emerging GTA-based artists originally came together for the project *The Complete Unknown*, curated by Marjan Verstappen at YTB (Younger Than Beyoncé) Gallery in Regent Park, Toronto, in 2016. In conversations with the AGO's Andrew Hunter, distinct ideas about Canada and identity emerged. This led to an invitation for the group to develop their own exhibition, housed within *Every. Now. Then: Reframing Nationhood.* Here, each individual artist or collective maintains their own distinct voice and identity. All have produced new works in response to this particular moment in Canada and Toronto, echoing and enhancing the critical ideas and themes of the larger exhibition.

Britta B.

I think we need affirmation. There's a lot of negative self-talk, at least for me and a lot of people I work with. It's easier to talk badly to ourselves. I want people to know they deserve to be cared for: that you must take care of yourself, take time for yourself, replenish yourself, and remind yourself of the good things that you are.

Fluke, 2017
Poetry and installation
(stool, table, bucket, and mixed media),
dimensions variable
Courtesy of the artist
Photo by Jason Hennessy

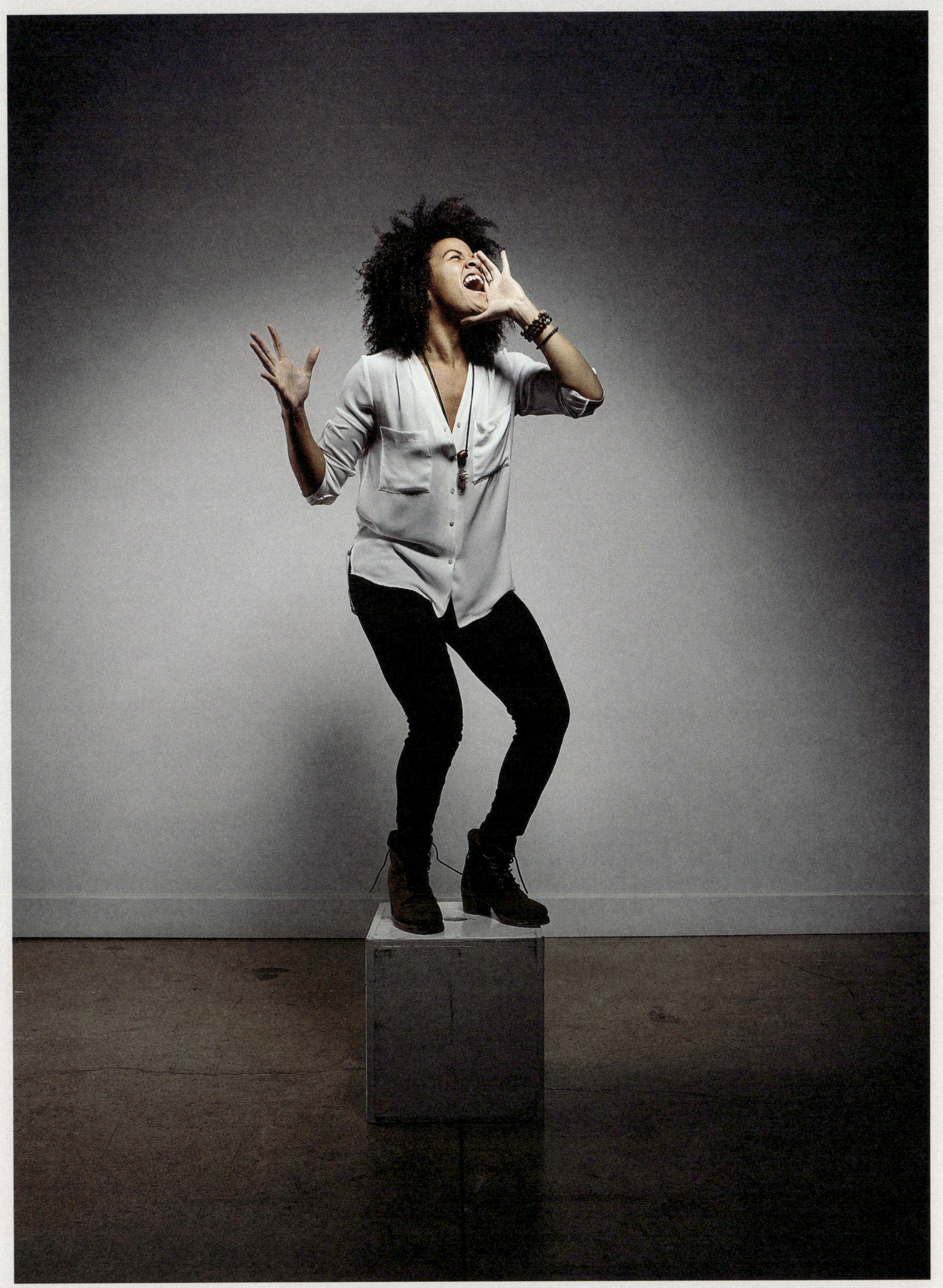

Topher Kong

I moved to Canada six years ago with my mom and my sister. When we arrived, we brought lots of luggage. I think of luggage as a representation of the journey, the hopes and expectations of a new life in a new country. At the same time, I think luggage carries memory, and represents the loss of the old life, too.

Yours/Your Father's/Your Mother's, 2017
Artist's rendering of installation, mixed media,
2 units, 304.8 × 200.7 × 38.1 cm each
Courtesy of the artist

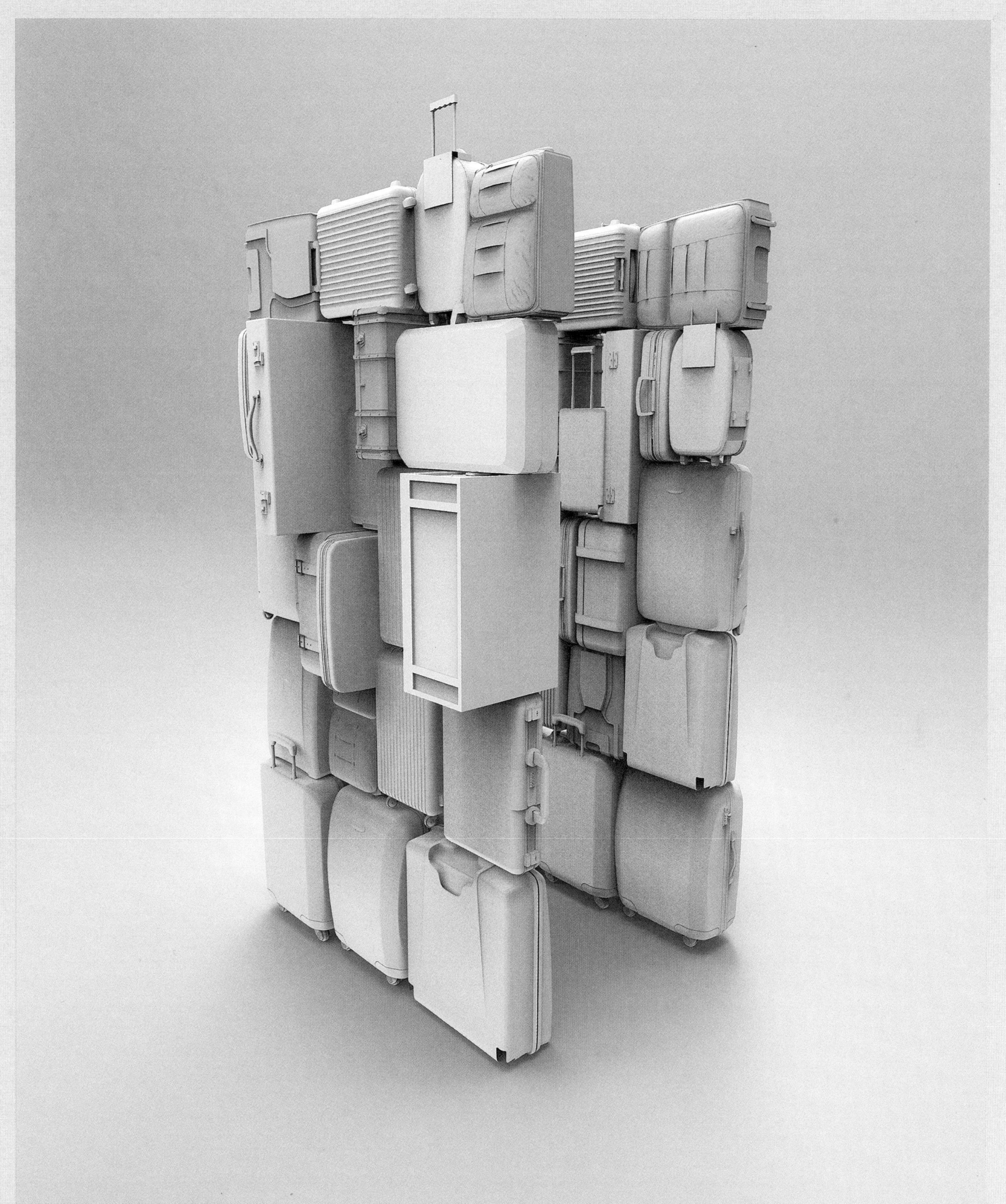

The moon's history is very similar to Canada's history—settlers really wanted to own it. I think this longing for alternate spaces to own and colonize is like a hope for a "new world." That's what brought people over to Canada. Settlers who came to Canada romanticized the land, and we still do that today—but we forget about who was here first. It is challenging to see Canada as 150 years old. As land and people's homes, it is much older. This is why I chose to depict the moon; it's part of everyone's landscape but impossible to own.

Man Has Reached Out and Touched the Tranquil Moon, 2017
Artist's rendering, clay bust with mask and projection, 22.9 × 22.9 × 61 cm
Courtesy of the artist

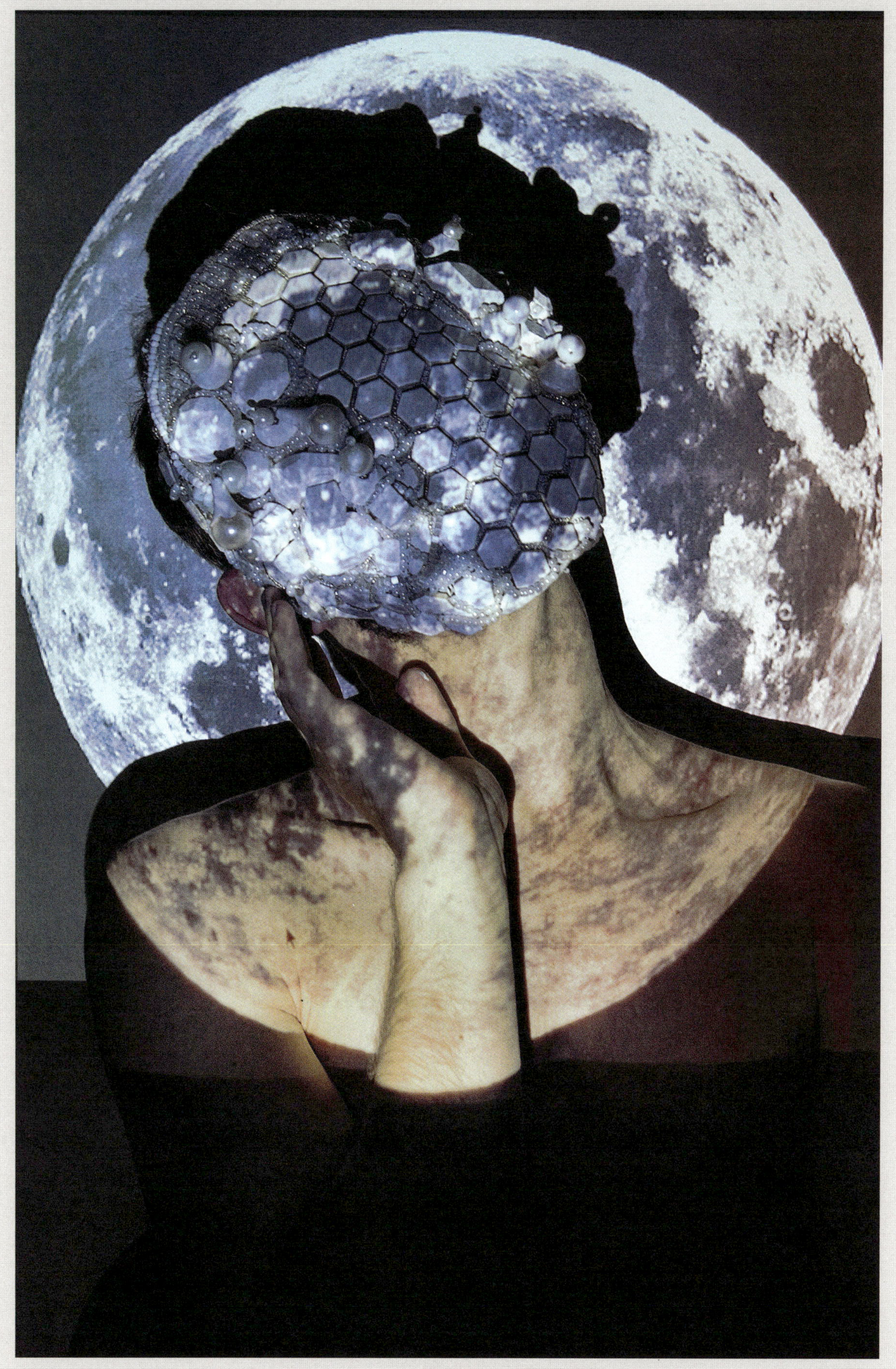

Sofia Mesa

I think of Canada's relations with Indigenous peoples, with refugees, and with non-status people as the moment before an arrow releases—the tension, the stretch... In the context of *this* 150 moment, my work is an exposure of those relations, literally and figuratively.

Episode 4, 2016
Production still
Courtesy of the artist

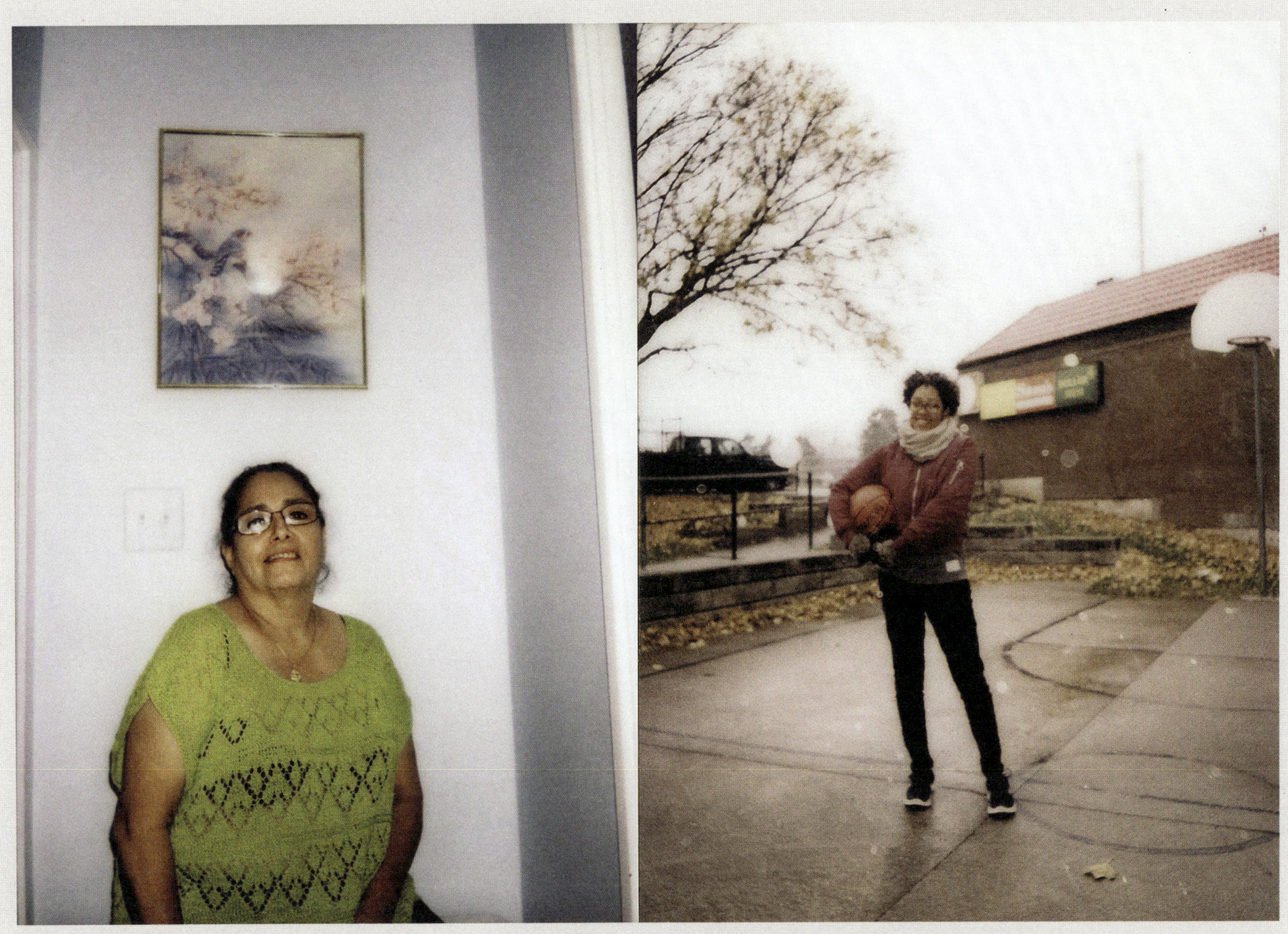

We're reflecting on our complicit role in the settler-colonial dialogue, and on our responsibility around shared space, cooperation, and reconciliation. As the state moves into celebratory reconciliation, we really need to address the truth before we think about reconciliation. If we want to be true allies, we need to actively listen.

—Pamila Matharu, Sister Co-Resister co-founder

Sister Co-Resister is Kiera Boult, Marilyn Fernandes, Ananda Gabo, Ashlee Harper, Shaista Latif, Sylvia Limbana, Pamila Matharu, Sofia Mesa, and Annie Wong.

Truth Before Reconciliation, 2017
Artists' rendering, mirrored chrome vinyl on black Plexiglas, 105.4 × 54.6 cm
Courtesy of the artist

Who's home on native land?

William Andrew Finlay Stewart

How do maps influence our ways of thinking? What structures do they enforce? Borders can be based on geographical features or be arbitrary, but they're drawn by those who hold power—imposed across land and between people.

Ambit, 2017
Research image for video installation
Courtesy of the artist

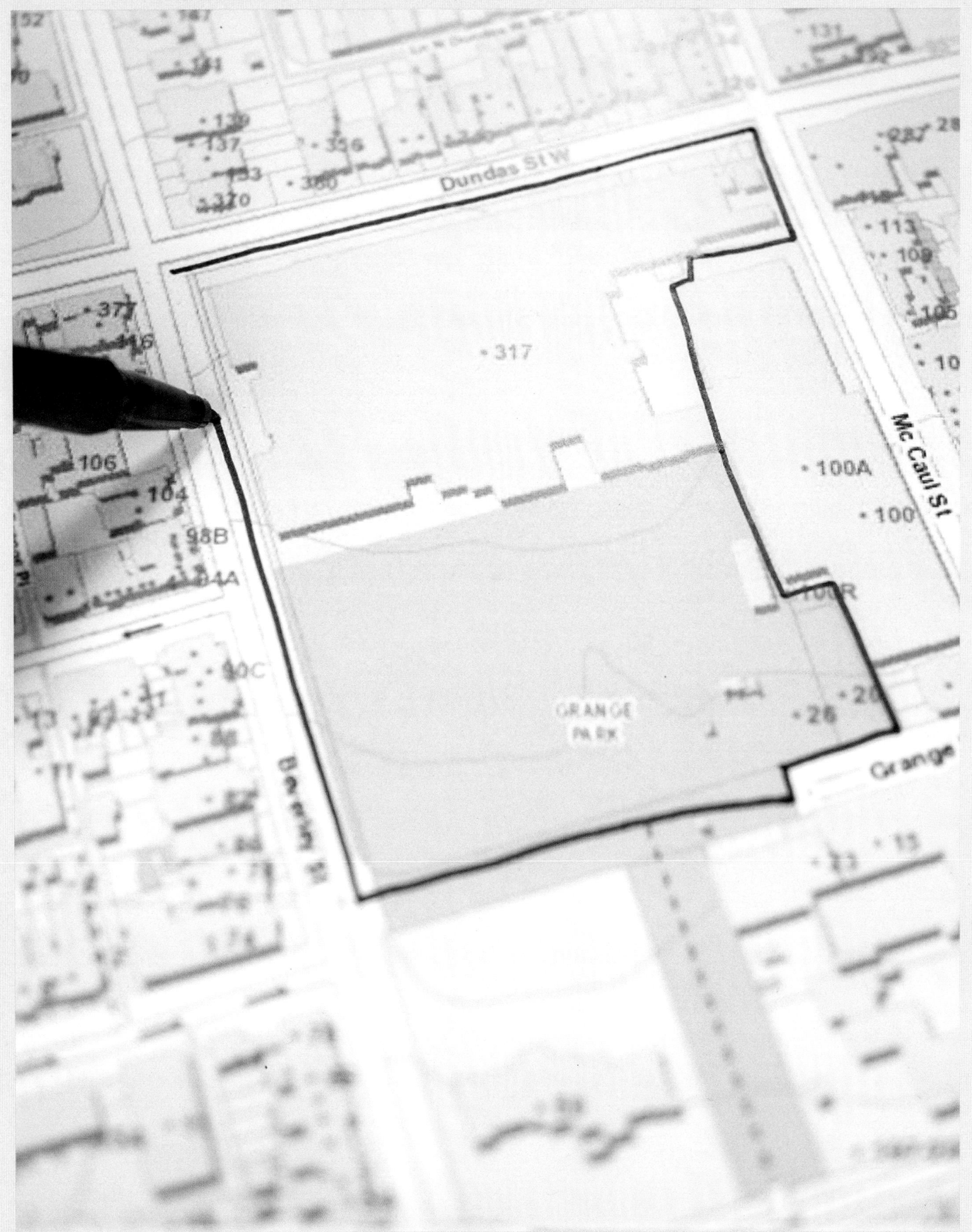
Dundas St W
317
Mc Caul St
100A
100
GRANGE
PARK
Grange

Ekow Stone

I think it's difficult to have this idea of pride and progress, and this Western Eurocentric uppity feeling and superiority complex. It's difficult for some of us to look back and see some pretty barbaric shit.

The Interpreter, 2017
Ink on paper, 30.5 × 22.9 cm
Courtesy of the artist

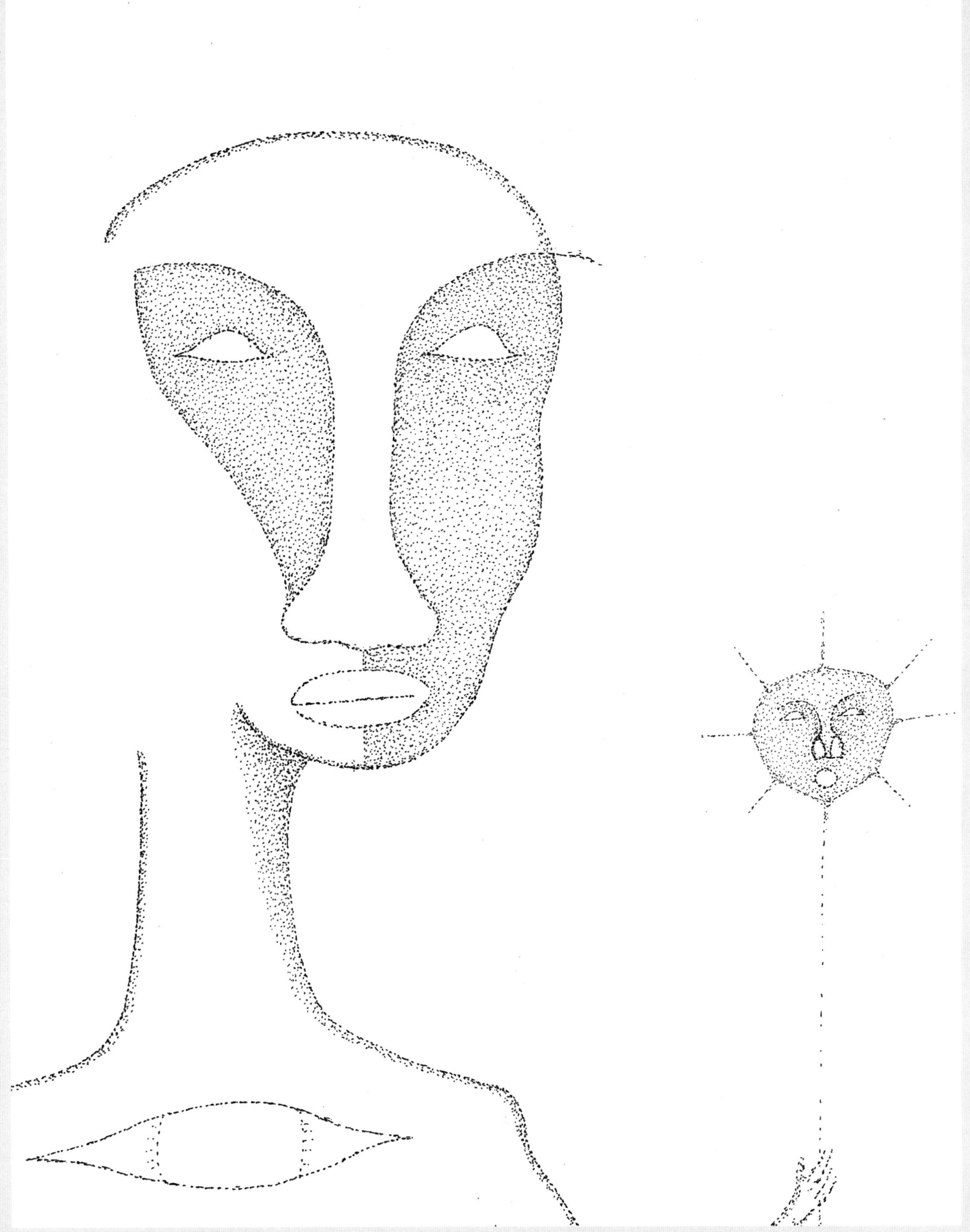

Marjan Verstappen

In the early 1600s, European surveyors began drawing maps of the land that would become Canada. These maps distort the stolen lands that Canada rests upon.

Dandelion seeds tie together the current moment in Canadian history with when European settlers began to control the land. My work re-imagines the moment when European surveyors came and transported these seeds from their clothes and bodies to different soil.

The Plot of Surveyor Colonel Dennis, 1869, 2017
Graphite on paper, 106.7 × 152.4 cm
Courtesy of the artist
Photo by the Art Gallery of Ontario

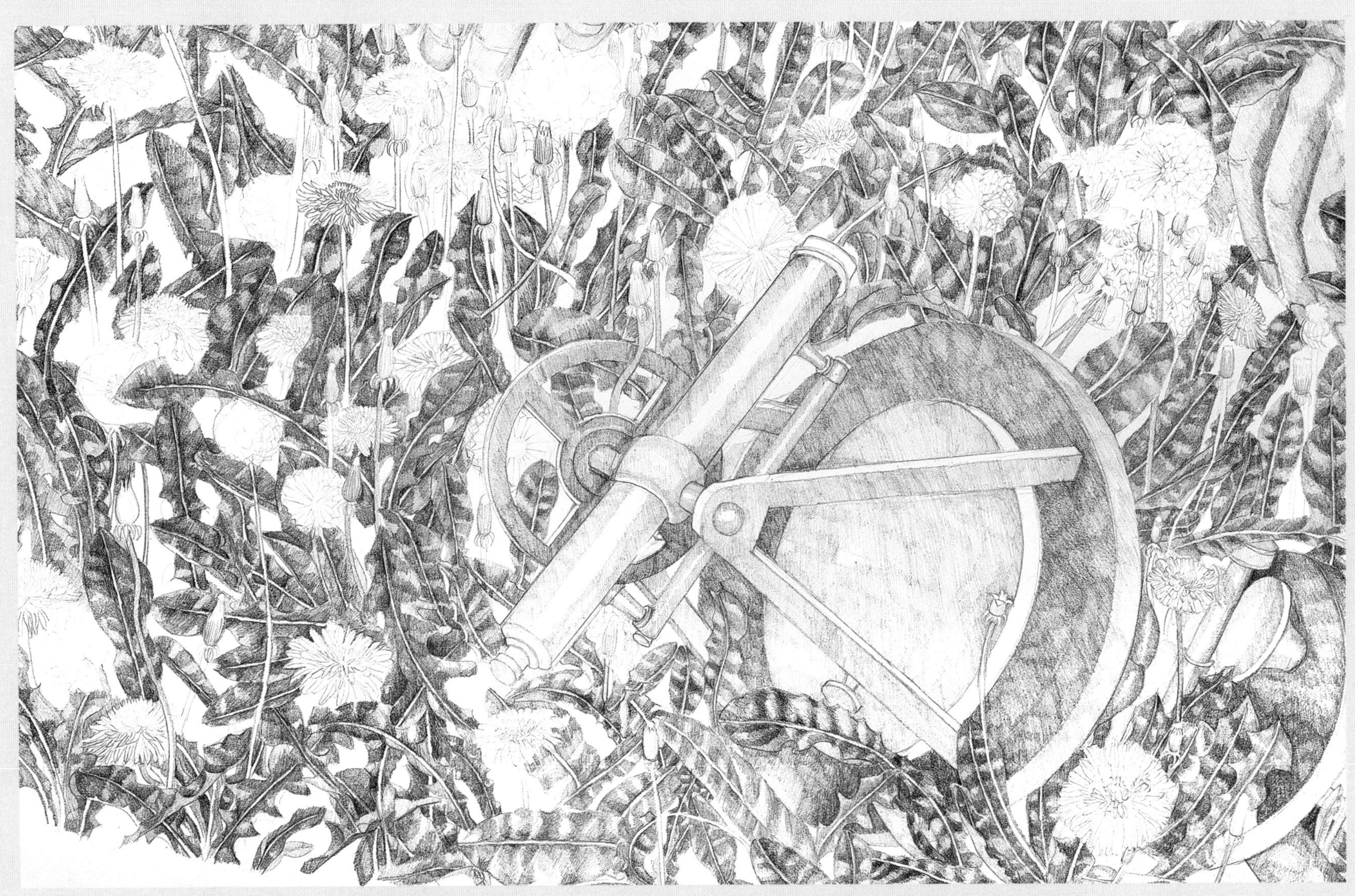

Essays

Hands Off!
On Indigenous Women's Love and Labour in the Institution

Quill Christie-Peters

Indigenous women's love is specific. Indigenous women's love is focused and powerful. It is the kind of love that binds the self, community, nation, homeland, and ancestors seamlessly to one another, and then nestles this entity into the greater web of creation. An Indigenous woman's love is endless, boundless, wildly imaginative. This love is such a strong force that it has been the target of settler colonialism since contact. This love is the core of Indigenous nationhood and is rooted in the specific places we come from. Early settlers knew they had to target this love in order to remove Indigenous bodies from their homelands, to secure the theft of land on which they would then impose their systems of white supremacy, capitalism, and heteropatriarchy that necessitate the ongoing dispossession of Indigenous peoples. And yet, the love of Indigenous women—and here the colonial context requires that I must clarify that I innately mean all those who identify as women—is unstoppable.

Throughout settler colonialism on Turtle Island, we have continued to love despite the genocide, the violence, and the dispossession that canada now seeks to celebrate. As an Anishinaabekwe, I refuse to mark anniversaries of attempted genocide. I refuse to participate in the national delusion and colonial amnesia that actively facilitate the contemporary dispossession of Indigenous land and bodies. As an Anishinaabekwe, I continue to love. I struggle to love in a world that teaches me to hate myself, to forget where my homeland is, to forget who my ancestors are, who so lovingly resisted and created so that I could do the same. This type of love, the kind that overflows the boundaries and hierarchies colonialism has so violently enforced, is horrifyingly threatening to the colonial objectives that define canada.

In the arts-based work that I do with Indigenous youth, love is the driving force that pushes me to bring every part of myself to the table. Within this work, we gather together and embody a relational praxis of art making that seeks to strengthen and reclaim the relationships that settler colonialism has sought to destroy. We gather to explore the relationships we have to the self, each other, our homelands, and our ancestors, and in doing so, we radically love ourselves, our communities, and the lands we come from. Initiating this type of work from within the Art Gallery of Ontario has been challenging—and here I remind you that major art institutions are pillars of capitalism that reproduce colonial myths and craft the comforting nationalist narratives that have allowed canada to turn a blind eye to its bloody roots. My love is the reason why I have, at times, worn myself thin and found myself in places of institutional hostility, spaces in which I had hoped never to be.

It is my willingness to stretch myself thin that makes my love visible to the institution. My love is then read by the institution as palatable, acceptable, and exploitable; as a means to extract my labour. The labour of "decolonizing the institution" can be extracted from me when, out of love, I am frantically trying to create safe space for Indigenous youth within the institution. The labour of building institutional sustainability can be extracted from me when, out of love, I am desperately trying to ensure that the position I have opened up for another Indigenous person is not as unsafe as it has been for me. The labour of translation weighs heavily on my shoulders when, out of love, I need to believe that this place can be transformed, even momentarily, in order for these beautiful young people to feel they are welcome in a place that has historically erased, excluded, and commodified their bodies. I am left an exhausted dichotomy, simultaneously the underqualified, should-be-grateful-for-the-opportunity, and willing-to-go-above-and-beyond decolonization expert.

Love is the core of certain forms of my labour. But make no mistake, even though I am extending, bending, and defending, my love remains uncompromising, unfaltering, and absolute. My love creates the boundaries of what I will not tolerate. In all of its ferocity, but, most of all, in its refusal to falter or be altered in any way, my love becomes unsettling, threatening, unreadable. I am no longer the palatable source of extractable labour and I am quickly cast as deviant and rebellious.

Ultimately the institution will never understand the type of love that I have for my community: the type that shatters the hierarchies that define power within the institution; the type that binds my body to the submerged homelands we were forced off, because of government flooding; the type that makes my life so beautifully meaningful, that despite all of the struggles, I always have purpose, I always have laughter, I always have the presence of my ancestors standing behind me. It is this type of love that is incomprehensible to capitalist logics, yet always recognized in its deviance. Our love makes institutions quake, makes the state tremble in fear; it always has. Our love causes a longing ache and deep sadness in those who live immersed within their compliance in upholding structures of oppression. So I am left tired and fugitive, but always immersed in love.

We find ourselves working within institutions for different reasons: some of us want to transform these spaces; some of us simply want to access space and resources; some of us cannot stand by and watch as large institutional/corporate complexes profit from stolen land without giving back a damn thing. I come to this place through an autonomous space model. This means, give us the space and resources you owe us and get out of the way.

At the end of the day, I have carved out the tiniest of spaces for young artists to fill with their own powerful, beautiful, and dynamic love. These young ones teach me that I have to love myself even more in these institutional spaces, that I need to remember that love must flow outwards and inwards, that an Indigenous woman loving herself is the deepest threat to colonialism. They teach me that self-love allows us to celebrate ourselves, our work, our bodies. They teach me that self-love in the institution means a refusal to accommodate, a refusal to translate, a refusal to accept paternalism, a refusal to cushion white fragility, and a refusal to cede control. Importantly—and the reason why I write this article—radical self-love in an institutional context means ownership and consent of my love and labour.

Celebrating 150 years of genocide and dispossession means that canada and its institutions hungrily search for Indigenous labour they can claim, consume, distort, and commodify. The optics and narratives of canada 150 are serious business. canada's weak fingers grasp for authenticity and legitimacy amidst a foundation of blatant injustice, genocide, slavery, and violence. I will not let my love and labour be claimed by the institution. As we move further into a national consciousness premised on the state-sanctioned reconciliation industry, I hope we can remember the centrality of Indigenous land and bodies in our explorations of how to exist in this place together. The future must be built with consent and must centre the repatriation of Indigenous land. At the very least, we need to be able to choose to access resources and space without the exhausting labour of creating, defending, and guarding those spaces. We have so much work to do, and canada, its institutions, the Art Gallery of Ontario, will never be privy to this work. Let us gather in these small autonomous spaces we work so hard to carve out. Let us exist within the fleeting moments where we are afforded due resources, and let us love. Let us love our communities, our nations, our homelands, and our ancestors until this love is enough to burn what has never served us to the ground.

Quill Christie-Peters is an Anishinaabekwe artist and youth arts programmer. A member of the Every. Now. Then. *curatorial team, she is a master's candidate in the Indigenous Governance Program at the University of Victoria. She lives in Toronto.*

Re-imagining the Enslaved
Eighteenth-Century Freedom Seekers as Twenty-First Century Sitters

Charmaine A. Nelson

Since at least the seventeenth century, Africans arrived in Canada in bondage. Their forcible relocation from Africa, or other parts of the Americas, was facilitated by their designation, first as cargo, and subsequently as chattel; a strategy that excluded them from the category of settler. That these histories—spanning over two hundred years and two empires (British and French)—are overwhelmingly disavowed is a result of Canada's national myth of racial tolerance and, concomitantly, the profound failures of Canada's education system. However, it does not take much digging to uncover the lie of our blinkered, heroic, national self-aggrandizement as the territory to which enslaved African Americans fled.[1]

On Tuesday, September 1, 1772, John Rock of Halifax, Nova Scotia, placed a fugitive notice in the *Nova-Scotia Gazette and the Weekly Chronicle* for an enslaved Black girl known as Thursday (Figure 1). Rock's notice for Thursday obscenely juxtaposed descriptions of her self-care and beautification practices (the red ribbon worn about her head) with what was almost assuredly evidence of her physical abuse (the lump above her right eye). The fugitive notices placed for Bell and Bett, both of whom briefly escaped captivity in Quebec, also convey something of the specific horrors of female enslavement (Figures 2–4). Bell's two documented escapes, less than three months apart, attest to the urgency of her desire to flee.[2] That she first ran away in August 1778, with "no shoes or stocking on," and fled again in October 1778, when fall temperatures made escape even more perilous, speaks to her desperation. But the conditions of Bett's escape were even more dramatic. When the approximately eighteen-year-old Bett escaped on the winter evening of March 7, 1787, the merchants Johnston and Purss described her as "big with child, and within a few days of her time"[3] (Figure 4).

Fast-forward to 2017, and Bell and Bett have been re-imagined: Bell as a stunning, caramel-coloured vision in a figure-flattering dress and stiletto heels, her gaze confidently confronting us for daring to interrupt her mid-phone call; and the exquisite seated Bett, eyes concealed behind fashionable dark sunglasses, showing off her beautiful, chocolate-coloured legs beneath her multi-coloured, ruffled skirt (Figures 5 and 6). But what does it mean to re-imagine these eighteenth-century enslaved freedom seekers as poised and beautiful, twenty-first century divas?[4]

The colonial archive of fugitive slave advertisements (including significant collections in Nova Scotia, Quebec, and Ontario) calls us to understand the retention of African self-care practices within the world of psychic, physical, and social abuse and material deprivation that was Transatlantic slavery. Through their innovative photographic reinterpretations of enslaved Africans in Canada, Camille Turner and Camal Pirbhai exploit this archive to provoke a conversation about Canada's role in Transatlantic slavery, the stolen potential of our enslaved ancestors, and the resilience of Canada's diverse African populations.

The fugitive or runaway slave advertisement provides for us a window into the lives and worlds of the enslaved. Frequently printed in weekly newspapers alongside other news and advertisements of transatlantic significance, such notices routinely incentivized the public's cooperation with the offer of rewards and the threat of judicial retribution. Ubiquitous across the Americas, each example was about the recapture of an individual, or individuals, who had fled, and as such, required that their owners share details that illuminated what made the runaways unique, both in manner and appearance.

Research on the enslaved poses several substantial problems for the researcher; not the least among them are the ways in which the colonial nature of the archive occludes the lives of people who were held in bondage. Since the enslaved were considered cargo, commodities, or

RAN away from her Maſter JOHN ROCK, on Monday the 18th Day of Auguſt laſt; a Negroe Girl named *Thurſday*, about four and an half feet high, broad ſett, with a Lump above her Right Eye: Had on when ſhe run away a red Cloth Petticoat, a red Baize Bed Gown, and a red Ribbon about her Head. Whoſoever may harbour ſaid Negroe Girl, or encourage her to ſtay away from her ſaid Maſter, may depend on being proſecuted according as the Law ſhall direct. And whoſoever may be ſo kind to take her up and ſend her home to her ſaid Maſter, ſhall be paid all Coſts and Charges, together with TWO DOLLARS Reward for their Trouble.

JOHN ROCK.

HALIFAX, Sept. 1ſt, 1772.

FIG 1 Fugitive notice for Thursday, placed by John Rock of Halifax, in the *Nova Scotia Gazette and Weekly Chronicle*, September 1, 1772.

chattel in economic and legal discourses, white slave owners and their surrogates strategically prohibited them from being recorded in registries, ledgers, and documents, which were used to individualize and humanize whites.

Such advertisements are what Graham White and Shane White have referred to as "the most detailed descriptions of the bodies of enslaved African Americans available."[5] I would argue that their contention also generally applies to the regions of the Americas that practiced the Transatlantic slave trade, particularly places where abolition predated the development of photography.[6] Displaced from their homelands and forced to take up the role of un-free labour in the Americas, enslavement severely impeded the ability of Africans to remember their histories, maintain their ethnic specificity, practice their cultures, and care for their bodies. This was strategic on the part of white colonialists and the slave-owning classes, and evident in the immediate implementation of slave practices—like branding and renaming—that were meant to break the enslaved from their sense of individuality, family, and ancestry.[7]

Indeed, as Marcus Wood contends, "Slavery, as a legal and economic phenomenon, was premised upon the denial of personality, and of a personal history, to the slave."[8] Furthermore, ruling-class whites deliberately developed the colonial archive in ways that allowed Africans to enter almost always as the objects or "stock" owned by another, and therefore as partial and incomplete entries. This disturbing fact—that the most detailed representations of the enslaved were produced by their owners—provokes a confrontation with the archive, not as an objective or neutral container of facts and information, but as a site through which the elite secured their power by determining who could be represented and in what fashion.

Reading the Runaway

> FOURTEEN DOLLARS Reward
> RUN-AWAY, on Sunday Night last [28 Feb.]... a Negro-Man, named ISHMAEL, about 36 Years of Age, and nearly 5 Feet 6 Inches high... his Face much pitted with the small Pox. He wants some of his Upper-fore Teeth, as likewise the first Joint of the fourth Finger of his left Hand; and besides, on the middle of his Right-Leg, he has a fresh Eschar from a Horse Kick lately received and cured.[9]

Ishmael, twice represented by Turner and Pirbhai, ran away from the Quebec City merchant John Turner Sr. at least three times: in July 1779, March 1784, and June 1788 (Figure 7). Re-imagined as a dignified modern-day dandy (Figure 8) and a dignified cape-wearing gentleman (Figure 9), his scarred, marked, disabled, and no doubt abused body has been represented as that of self-assured, confident men. While John Turner described Ishmael as possessing a "black and copper coloured mixt Complexion," the modern-day Ishmaels emerge in two decidedly

amuſement well directed Satire is ſure to give.

RAN AWAY from my ſervice, on Tueſday night the 18th inſtant, A Mulatto Negreſs named BELL. I do hereby promiſe a reward of FOUR DOLLARS to any perſon who will apprehend ſaid Negreſs and bring her to me, or lodge her in his Majeſty's gaol in Quebec. She wore when ſhe went away a ſtriped woollen jacket and petticoat, and had no ſhoes or ſtockings on. I do caution all perſons from harbouring ſaid Negreſs, as I am determined to puniſh any perſon in whoſe cuſtody ſhe may be found to the utmoſt rigour of the law.

QUEBEC, Auguſt 19, 1778. GEO: HIPPS.

Triton, Thomas Byrne, —— Ditto.

ADVERTISEMENTS.

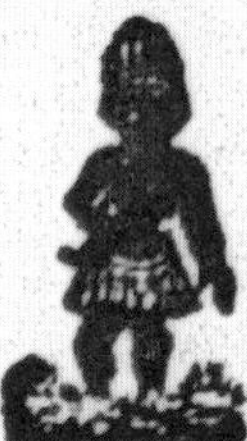

RUN away from Mr. GEORGE HIPPS on Thurſday laſt, a Mulatto wench named *BELL*, this is to give notice, that any perſon or perſons whatſoever who harbours the ſaid Girl may depend that he will go to the utmoſt rigour of the Law. When ſhe went away ſhe had upon her a Callico Gown and Petticoat, a dreſs'd Cap, and a black ſilk Handkerchief.

QUEBEC, *November* 3, 1778.

N. B. The ſubſcribers have alſo to let, that pleaſant Houſe on the hill, (either together or ſeparately) now occupied by Meſſrs. *Dorion* and *Sarjeant*.

Quebec, 6th March, 1787.

RAN-AWAY from the ſubſcribers, between the hours of ſeven and eight o'clock yeſterday evening, a NEGRO WENCH named BETT, about eighteen years old, middle ſtature, ſpeaks the Engliſh, French and German languages well; had on when ſhe went away, a blue Kerſey Jacket and Pettycoat, a dark cotton Cap with yellow ſtrings, and an Indian Shawl round her neck, was big with child, and within a few days of her time.

Whoever will apprehend ſaid Negreſs, and ſecure her return, ſhall be paid A REWARD of TWENTY DOLLARS, and all reaſonable expences.

Any perſon who may harbour or conceal the ſaid Negreſs, will be proſecuted to the rigour of the law, by JOHNSTON & PURSS.

For SALE *by* AUCTION *on the Premiſes*,

FIG 2 Fugitive notice for Bell, placed by Geo. Hipps in the *Quebec Gazette*, August 20, 1778.

FIG 3 Fugitive notice for Bell, placed by Geo. Hipps in the *Quebec Gazette*, November 5, 1778.

FIG 4 Fugitive notice for Bett, placed by Johnston and Purss in the *Quebec Gazette*, March 8, 1787.

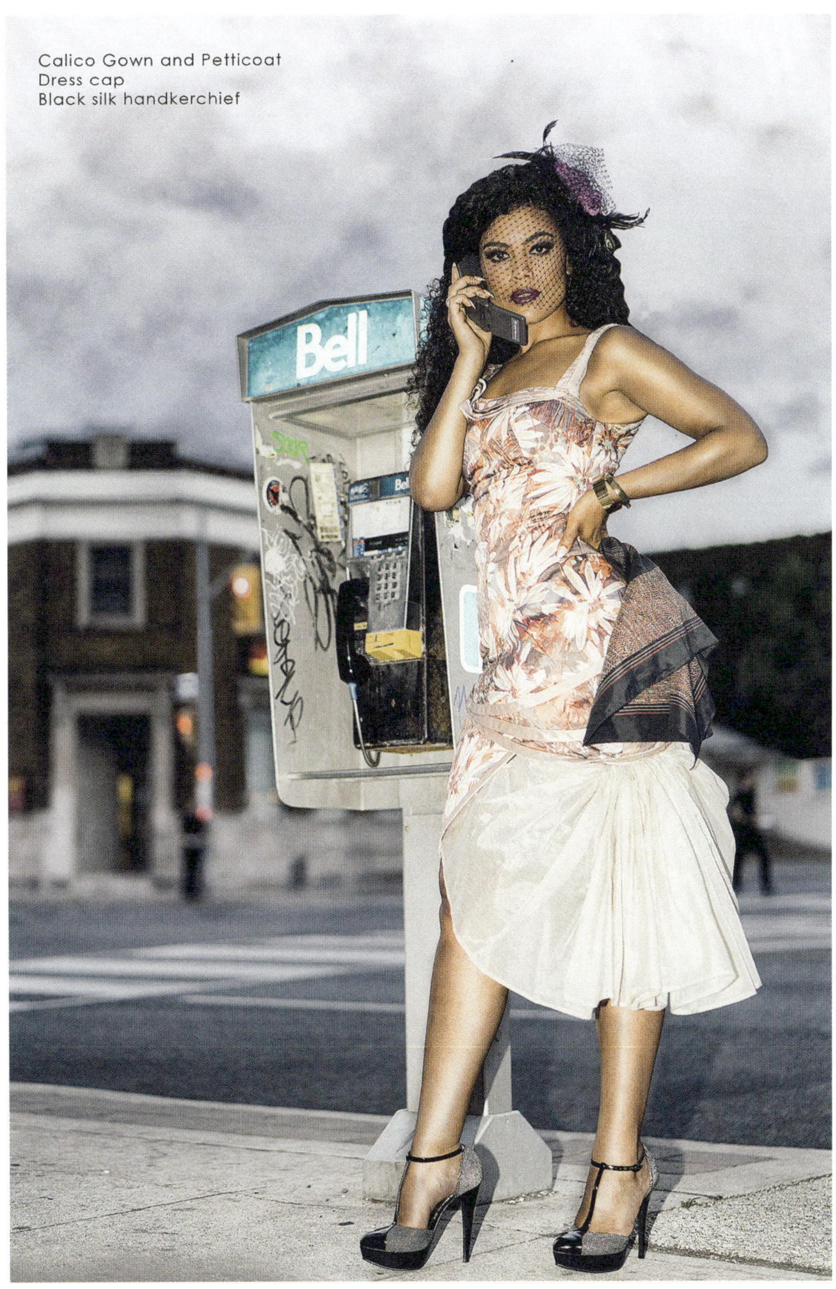

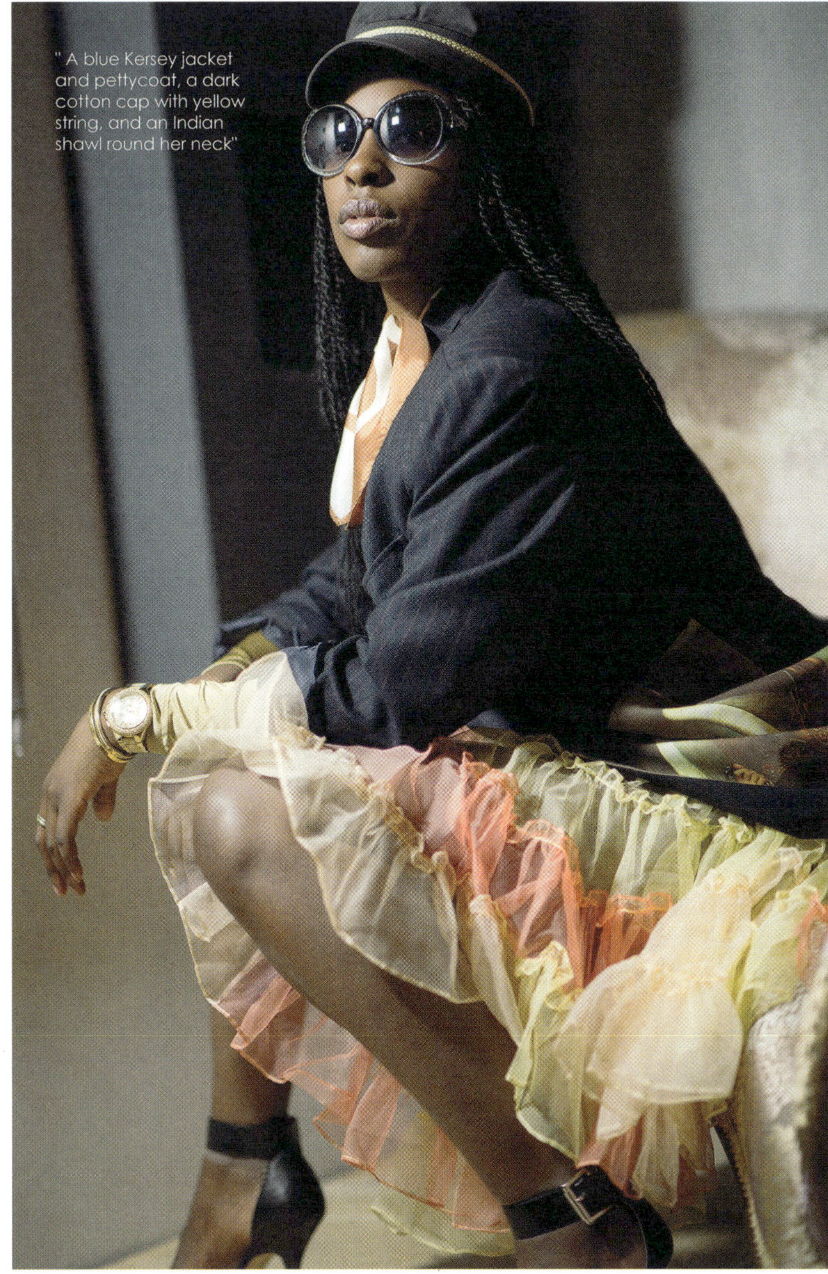

FIG 5 Camille Turner and Camal Pirbhai, *Bell,* from the *Wanted* series, 2016. Courtesy of the artists. Photo by Christina Sideris.

FIG 6 Camille Turner and Camal Pirbhai, *Bett,* from the *Wanted* series, 2016. Courtesy of the artists. Photo by Christina Sideris.

Sign'd at Quebec, March 2d, 1784. *44th Regiment.*

FOURTEEN DOLLARS REWARD.

RUN-AWAY, on Sunday Night laſt, from the Subſcriber, a Negro-Man, named ISHMAEL, about 36 Years of Age, and nearly 5 Feet 6 Inches high; of a remarkably down-caſt Countenance, and a black and copper coloured mixt Complexion; his Hair is ſhort, ſtrong black and curly; and his Face much pitted with the ſmall Pox. He wants ſome of his Upper-fore Teeth, as likewiſe the firſt Joint of the fourth Finger of his left Hand; and beſides, on the middle of his Right-Leg, he has a freſh Eſchar from a Horſe Kick lately received and cured: had on when he went off, a round Hat cocked up behind and a blue ſilk Band; a red pluſh Waiſtcoat; a pair of blue Bath coating Leggings and Breeches in one; and a Pair of Shoes and Metal Buckles.

He came from Claverac near Albany in 1776, with his former Maſter, C. Spencer; can ſpeak and read Engliſh tolerably well, and underſtands a little Dutch and French: he paſſes himſelf, 'tis ſaid, as a Free Negro, the more eaſily to effect unoticed his intended Eſcape out of the Province. Whoever will apprehend the ſaid Negro-Man, and deliver him to the Subſcriber, Merchant, Montreal, ſhall receive the above Reward, and all reaſonable Charges, from

JOHN TURNER.

Montreal, March 1, 1784.

FIG 7 Fugitive notice for Ishmael, placed by John Turner in the *Quebec Gazette,* March 11, 1784.

distinct hues—a move that challenges the authority with which whites laid claim to a knowledge of black bodies.[10] Gone is the "old Hat bedawbed with white Paint" (1779) and the pox-marked face.[11] Instead, the twenty-first-century Ishmaels exude confidence as both composure and self-possession.

While the most obvious glimpse of the original eighteenth-century Ishmael's ability to take control of his appearance arguably resides in the change in John Turner's description of his hairstyle—from "wears his own Hair which is black, long and curly" (1779),[12] to "his Hair is short, strong black and curly" (1784),[13] and finally to "black short curled hair" (1788)—the portraits of the re-imagined Ishmaels leave no doubt about who controls their likenesses.[14] Although Turner and Pirbhai are staging our epic re-encounters with enslaved freedom fighters, their fashionable, confident namesakes appear to have more in common with models in contemporary fashion magazines than with the enslaved people who navigated what Trevor Burnard has called "radical uncertainty."[15] The power of this potential reincarnation is that it allows us to think not only about what John Turner stole from Ishmael (his labour, years of his life, his access to self-determination), and how John Turner imagined and wanted to see Ishmael, but also how Ishmael, liberated from bondage, may have imagined and represented himself.

Fugitive Slave Advertisements as Portraits

What is called for is a rereading of fugitive slave advertisements not as mere texts but as *portraits,* however questionable, that function primarily through vision. However, the reconceptualization of fugitive slave advertisements as portraits of the enslaved is not a seamless fit for several reasons. First, while traditional "high" art portraiture—like that produced in marble or oil paint—was the end-product of a contract between a patron and an artist for a *flattering* likeness, the representations of enslaved fugitives generated by slave owners were designed to normalize slavery and to criminalize the enslaved for what Marcus Wood has termed "an act of theft, albeit a paradoxical self-theft"[16] (Figure 10).

Second, while in the traditional relationship the sitter and the patron were often one and the same, with fugitive notices the slave owner was the patron and creator of the notice, and the sitter was an unwilling participant in their representation. Third, while the artistic term for the represented subject in a portrait—the sitter—expresses the stillness required in the actual process of capturing a human likeness, a fugitive's escape was characterized by their self-directed motion, something that was literally coded as illegal under colonial law. Therefore, the portrait of the enslaved person that a fugitive slave advertisement captured was not of a stationary person—a sitter—but instead, of a person in motion, a runner.

Finally, since a fugitive's likeness was published against their will, these portraits were "stolen" and unauthorized. Yet they were also "fugitive" in the sense that they were elusive and often highly false images. They were false in the sense that slave owners deliberately vilified the character of the enslaved in the advertisements they placed, and could often not comprehend or accurately describe the African cultural practices of the enslaved. Furthermore, the commonality of fugitive tactics—like altering one's appearance or changing clothing to "pass" as another social group (mainly free people) in an age when most poor people had only one set of clothing—meant that the enslaved often did not precisely match their descriptions.

The medium of these printed portraits was text, as opposed to images, but the words were often strategically deployed with the goal of creating a mental image of the enslaved. Besides the height, weight, and clothing of the fugitive, such notices regularly recounted bodily marks. Ishmael is a case in point. The legalization of corporal punishment within colonial law meant that the bodies of the enslaved were commonly riddled with signs of violence. But the exposure of slave-owner violence in the description of the enslaved person's injured and tortured body—seen as necessary to the economic ends of the advertisement—signalled the moment in which the fugitive notice became a weapon against the slave-owning classes. As Wood explains, "the runaway emerges as a metaphor for white moral failure."[17]

Conclusion

Returning to my original question, what is the meaning of such a deliberate re-imagination? Decked out in the most fashionable clothing, beautiful, charismatic, and self-possessed, these re-imagined subjects are no longer oppressed, frightened, hunted, and terrorized. They exude confidence, delight in frivolity, and embrace luxury—things not afforded their namesakes. By insisting that Bell, Bett, and Ishmael were not slaves,

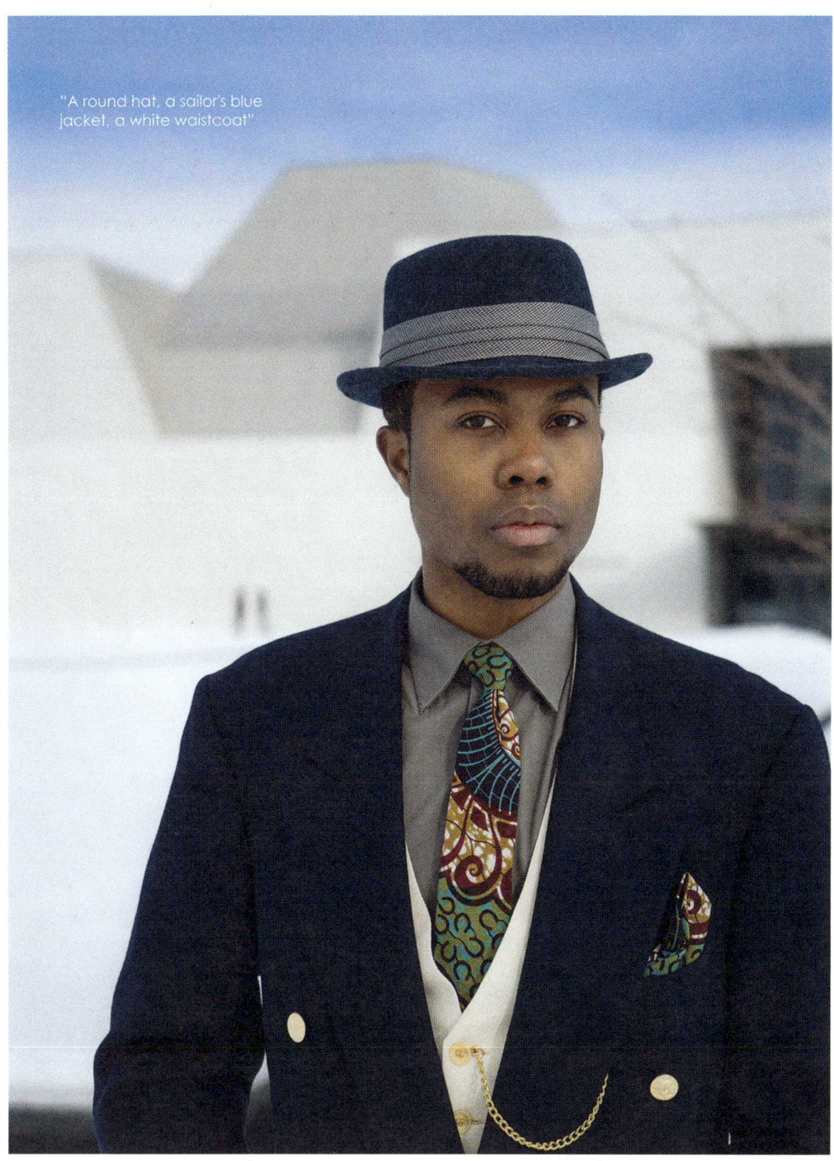

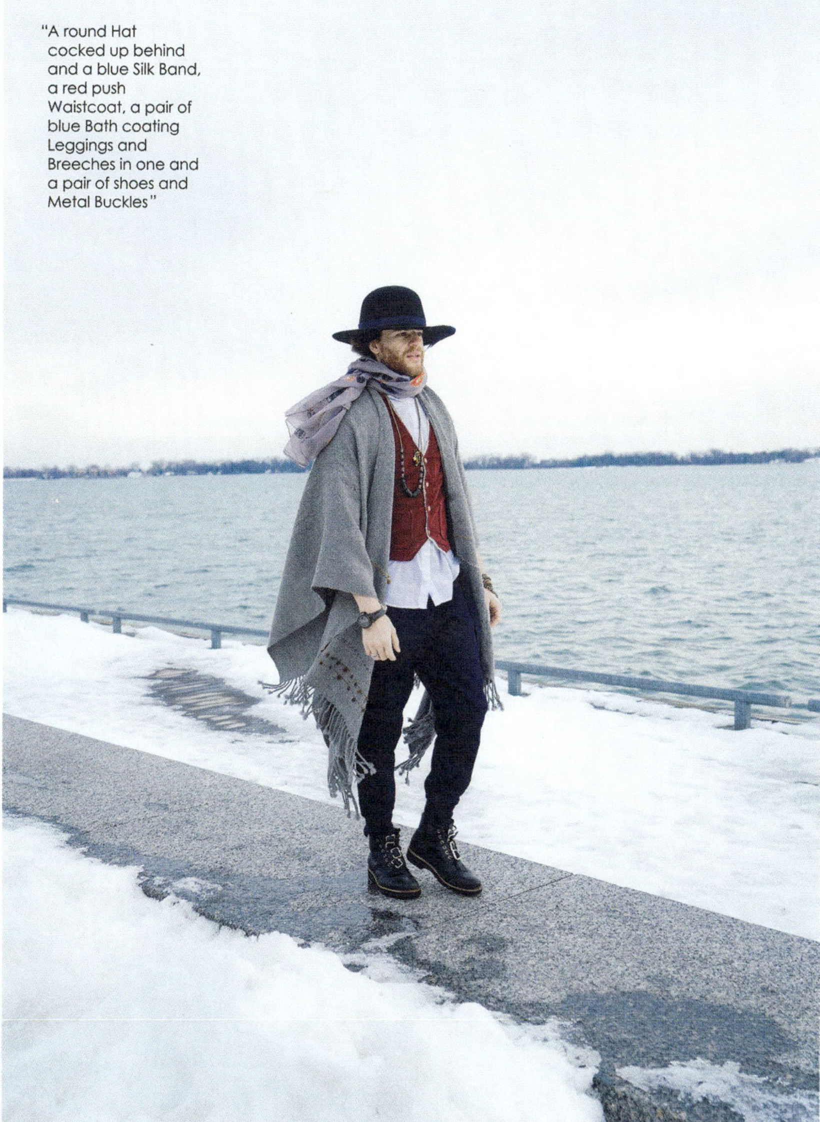

FIG 8 Camille Turner and Camal Pirbhai, *Ishmael,* from the *Wanted* series, 2017. Courtesy of the artists. Photo by Christina Sideris.

FIG 9 Camille Turner and Camal Pirbhai, *Ishmael,* from the *Wanted* series, 2017. Courtesy of the artists. Photo by Christina Sideris.

but *en*slaved—not possessions, but humans—we can see in their desire for freedom, as documented in their eighteenth-century fugitive notices, their heroism. This heroism resides not only in their literal quests for freedom but in their insistence that their bodies were their own, to be dressed (Thursday's red ribbon), styled, coiffed (Ishmael's cropped hair), and beautified as they—and not the slave owners—saw fit.

As Canadians reflect on the 150th anniversary of our nation, it behooves us to challenge the customary image of a homogeneously white Canada, one that strategically excludes the memory of Canadian participation in Transatlantic slavery and erases the centuries-long presence of people of African descent. Through the re-imagining of Bell, Bett, Ishmael, and other valiant freedom seekers, Camille Turner and Camal Pirbhai challenge us to think anew about the tremendous importance of integrating the memory and histories of Black Canada into our national narrative.

Dr. Charmaine A. Nelson holds a Ph.D. in Art History from the University of Manchester. A professor at McGill University, she lives in Montreal. Her book Slavery, Geography, and Empire in Nineteenth-Century Marine Landscapes of Montreal and Jamaica *was published in 2016.*

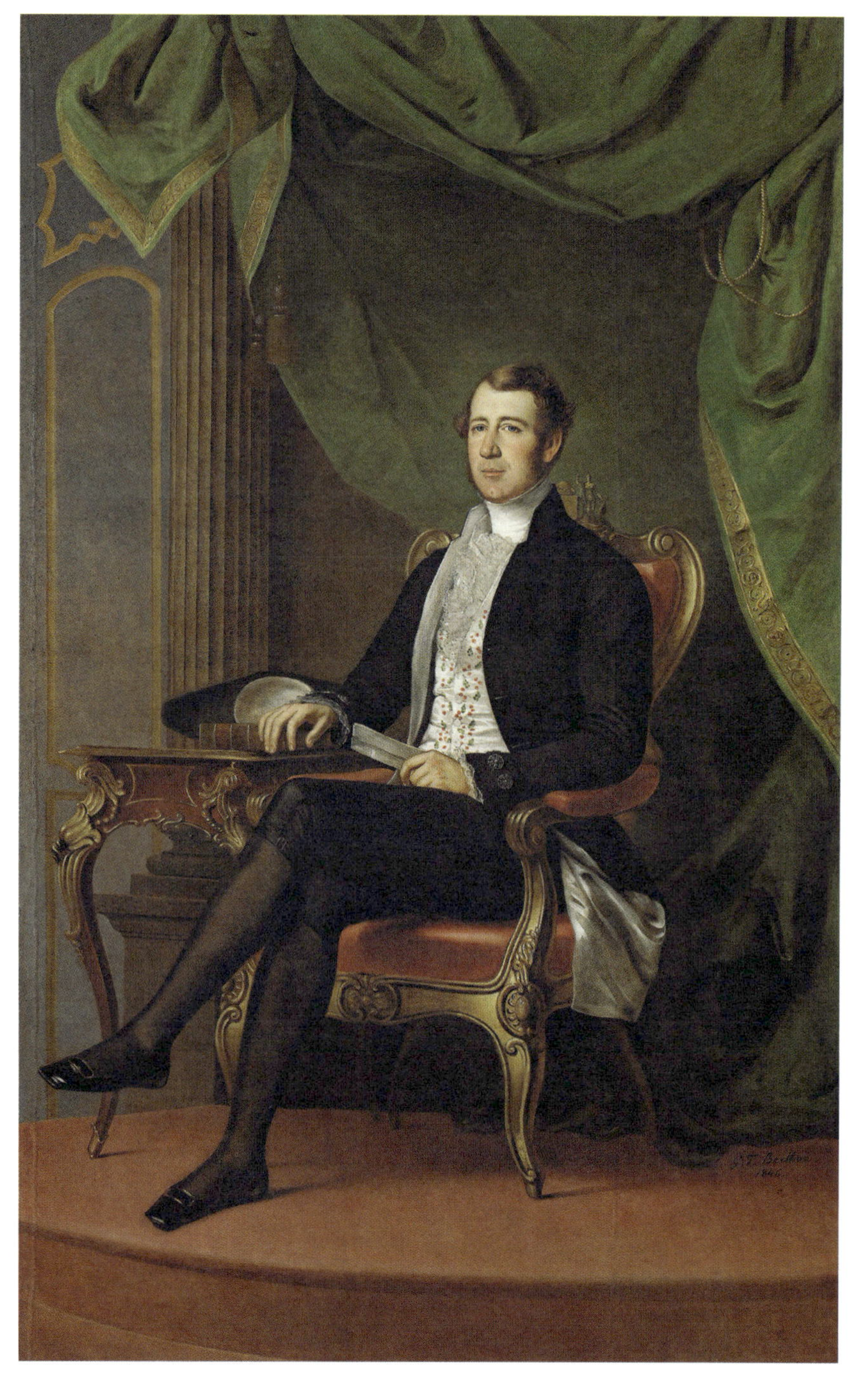

FIG 10 George Theodore Berthon, *Portrait of William Henry Boulton*, 1846. Oil on canvas, 240.5 × 147.5 cm. Collection of the Art Gallery of Ontario, The Goldwin Smith Collection, GS111.

NOTES

1. "Heritage minutes: Underground railroad," *Historica Canada* website, video; released 1991. The focus on Canada as a land of abolitionism only, has been assisted by the circulation of popular representations like "Heritage Minutes: Underground Railroad."

2. George Hipps, "RAN AWAY from my service," *Quebec Gazette*, August 20, 1778; and, "RUN away from Mr George Hipps," *Quebec Gazette,* November 5, 1778; reproduced in Frank Mackey, "Appendix I: Newspaper Notices," in *Done with Slavery: The Black Fact in Montreal, 1760–1840* (Montreal: McGill-Queen's University Press, 2010), 321.

3. James Johnston and John Purss, "RAN-AWAY from the subscribers," *Quebec Gazette,* March 8, 1787; in Mackey, "Appendix I: Newspaper Notices," 329.

4. I am grateful to Sylvia Hamilton for sharing with me her idea of enslaved fugitives as freedom-runners; conversation between Sylvia Hamilton and the author, November 7, 2015, Halifax, Nova Scotia.

5. Graham White and Shane White, "Slave Hair and African American Culture in the Eighteenth and Nineteenth Centuries," *Journal of Southern History,* 61, no. 1 (February 1995): 49.

6. Laird W. Bergad, *The Comparative Histories of Slavery in Brazil, Cuba, and the United States* (Cambridge: Cambridge University Press, 2007), xiii. Two places where the fugitive slave archive may pale in comparison to photographic archives of the enslaved are Cuba and Brazil, where slavery was not abolished until 1886 and 1888 respectively. For more on photography of the enslaved in Brazil see Margrit Prussat, "Icons of Slavery: Black Brazil in Nineteenth-Century Photography and Image Art," *Living History: Encountering the Memory of the Heirs of Slavery,* ed. Ana Lucia Araujo (Newcastle upon Tyne: Cambridge Scholars Publishing, 2009).

7. Ira Berlin, "From Creole to African: Atlantic Creoles and the Origins of African-American Society in Mainland North America," *William and Mary Quarterly,* Third Series, 53, no. 2 (April 1996): 251–52. The Virginia planter, Robert "King" Carter (the richest planter in the state), who owned a plantation on the Rappahannock River, instructed his overseer to initiate a process of renaming his enslaved Africans at the point of purchase.

8. Marcus Wood, "Rhetoric and the Runaway: The Iconography of Slave Escape in England and America," in *Blind Memory: Visual Representations of Slavery in England and America, 1780–1865* (Manchester: Manchester University Press, 2000), 87.

9. John Turner, "FOURTEEN DOLLARS reward, RUN-AWAY, on Sunday night last," *Quebec Gazette,* March 11, 1784, in Mackey, "Appendix I: Newspaper Notices," 326.

10. Ibid.

11. Turner, "TEN DOLLARS REWARD," *Quebec Gazette,* July 29, 1779; in Mackey, "Appendix I: Newspaper Notices," 322.

12. Ibid., 321. The particular phrasing of this statement is also important because it discloses that black males wore wigs at this juncture. A later advertisement for the capture of "a Negro" William Spencer noted that he wore "a round hat and generally a wig." Jacob Kuhn and EDW. WM. Gray, "BROKE goal and escaped on Sunday the 18th," *Montreal Gazette,* November 22, 1792; in Mackey, "Appendix I: Newspaper Notices," 335.

13. Turner, "FOURTEEN DOLLARS reward," in Mackey, "Appendix I: Newspaper Notices," 326.

14. John Turner, Senior, "RUN away from the subscriber," *Quebec Gazette,* June 26, 1788; in Mackey, "Appendix I: Newspaper Notices," 331. Ishmael's dramatic change in hairstyle may have been a tactic to evade recapture, but equally, since African haircare was largely communal, the shorter hair may have been a practical consideration for a man enslaved in a slave minority community.

15. Trevor Burnard, "The Sexual Life of an Eighteenth-Century Jamaican Slave Overseer," in *Sex and Sexuality in Early America,* ed. Merril D. Smith (New York: New York University Press, 1998), 165.

16. Wood, "Rhetoric and the Runaway," 79.

17. Ibid., 82.

Every. Now. Then.
Of Impacts, Migrations, and Erratics
Andrew Hunter

At first it is hard to read the image, hard to discern what lies below the *Canadarm*—the iconic limb that has appeared consistently in articulations of Canadian pride since it first extended its reach from the Space Shuttle *Columbia* in November of 1981—which now stretches out from the lower left of the frame, out from the International Space Station's cargo bay. In April 2001, Canadian astronaut Chris Hadfield drifted out into space—perhaps on his spacewalk—and now, via this photograph (Figure 1, right), we glide with him in orbit over northern Quebec. The robotic limb points to a circle embossed on the earth—a pockmark, bullet hole, wound, what some will read as an eye. The familiar orientation is rotated: "up" (north) is lower right, west is now up, the St. Lawrence cuts the image in half. The large island in the gulf is Anticosti (L'île-d'Anticosti), a name possibly derived from the Innu word *natiscotec,* meaning "where bears are hunted."[1]

51° 23′ N, 68° 42′ W—this wound is Lake Manicouagan, another Innu term meaning "where tree bark is found."[2] Look into the eye. The land at the centre is René-Levasseur Island; its tallest peak is Mount Babel. *Babel* or *Babylon,* recalling the mythical Tower of Babel built by a collective humanity who shared culture, spoke the same tongue, but dared to reach for a shared conception of Heaven, only to be dispersed by an angry God who released a deluge—a God who chose to confound their efforts by creating multiple languages, then scattering them across the globe, seeding discord.

René-Levasseur Island was named for Hydro-Québec's chief engineer who oversaw the construction of the Daniel-Johnson Dam in 1970, and the lake that surrounds the island is the reservoir formed by the damming of the Manicouagan River. The dam was named for Daniel Johnson Sr., premier of Quebec from 1966 to 1968 (whose sons would also be premiers in the 1980s and 1990s). Before the dam there was no island, just two crescent-shaped lakes. The dam flooded the land and revealed the crater, making it visible from space, from deep space, where a five-kilometre diameter bolide came hurtling, 215.5 million years out.

When it meets us, the continents are still fused as Pangaea (Figure 2, right), a supercontinent that has not yet begun to rift apart, disperse, and diversify. It's hot and dry. The only tree bark you can find is coniferous. There are no bears to hunt, but cynodonts abound. Western science tells us that this is the Late Triassic. (That's just one explanation—there are more names, more layers of meaning, more stories to tell, between this place here and now and us.) The Triassic begins over 250 million years out with the largest mass extinction in the earth's history. The Great Permian Extinction is also known as the Great Dying because over 90% of life on earth is wiped out. The Triassic-Jurassic event closes the Triassic. Three-quarters of all life is exterminated and the age of dinosaurs is ushered in; an era that ultimately ends when another celestial body collides with the earth at 66 million years. The Cretaceous-Paleogene (K-Pg) extinction event leaves a massive 180 kilometre-wide impact crater (or astrobleme) beneath the Yucatán Peninsula and the Gulf of Mexico: the Chicxulub crater, a Yucatec Mayan word meaning "tick-devil" or "the well of the great horns."[3] Do all those horned beings still prowl beneath us?

The world turns, the sun passes over, and the eye of Lake Manicouagan blinks back. I am looking at maps, images, and renderings, moving through and over time, not back in time, but into a pool of deep time—where a past that awaits us in the future was here before us, and with us, always. Everything expands and contracts, turns back on itself. Every Now *is* Then, and Then *is* Now, and what *Then*?

In 1867, a blip, Canada emerges as a country, but not the country as it is now, just a thin wedge—Ontario and Quebec (formerly Upper and Lower Canada), plus two Maritime provinces (Nova Scotia and New Brunswick), all huddled around the St. Lawrence gulf, the northern border marked by the height of land. Beyond this point, water flows north to James Bay. Such a tiny event within this vast pool of time, beings, and forces; just a

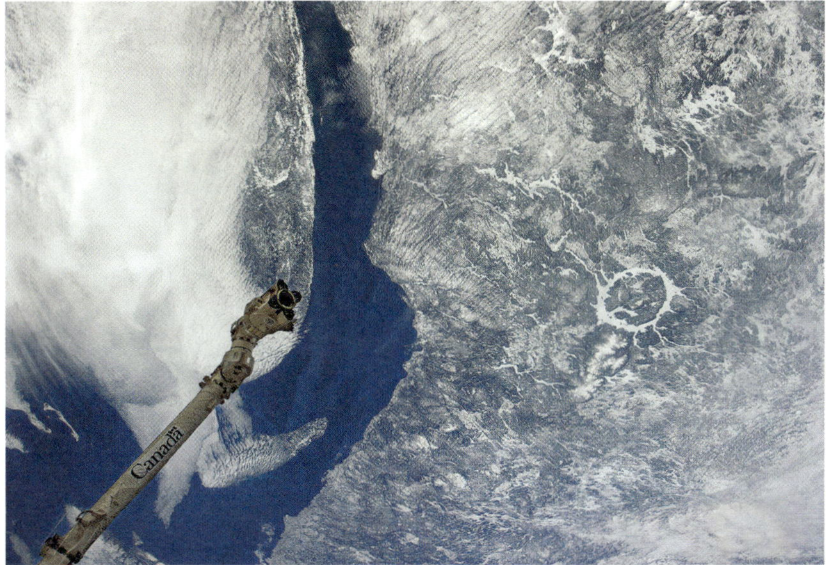

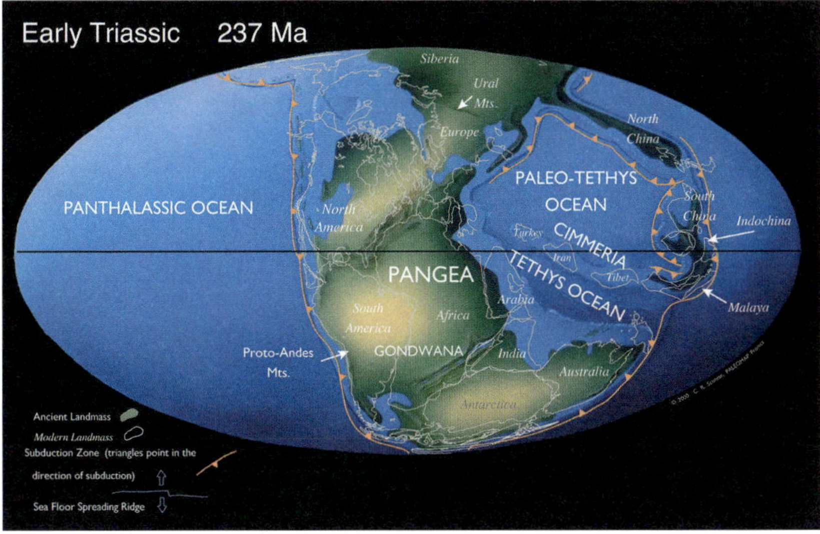

FIG 1 CANADARM2 and Lake Manicouagan. © Courtesy of the Canadian Space Agency.

FIG 2 Triassic paleogeographic map by C.R. Scotese.

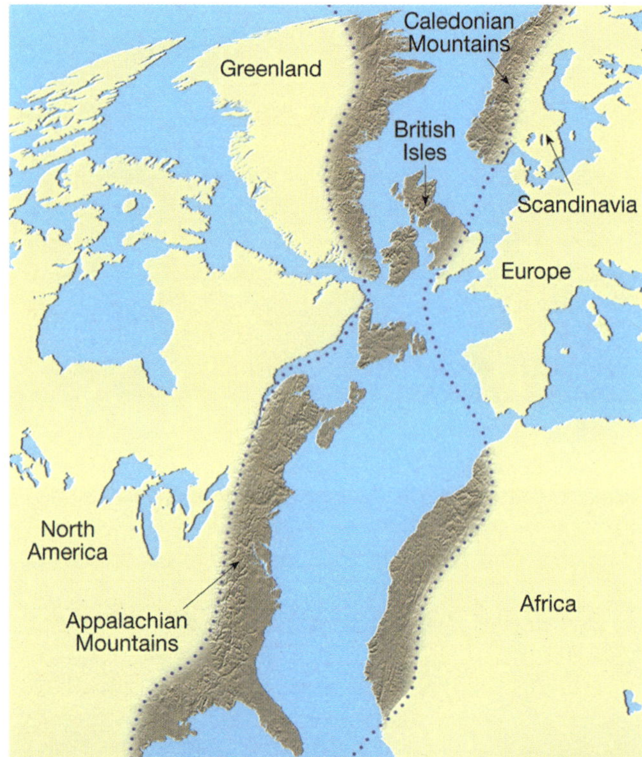

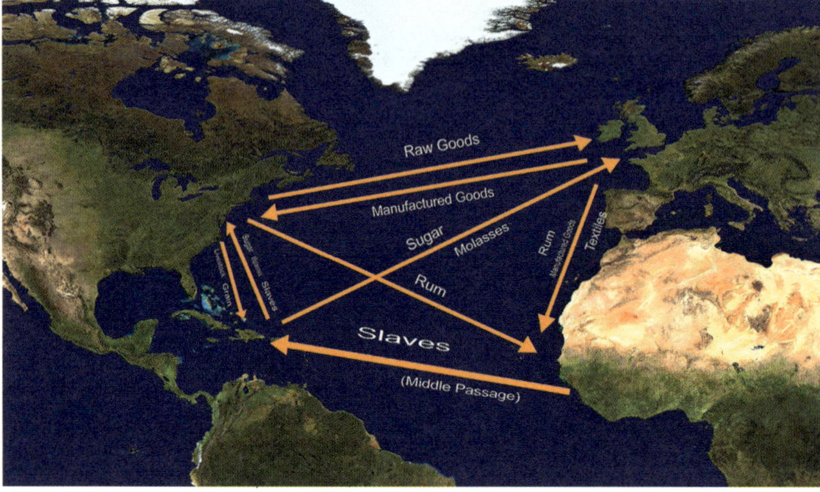

FIG 3 The presence of identical rock on the east coast of North America and the west coast of Europe, evidence of the ancient supercontinent Pangaea. © 2009 Tasa Graphic Arts, Inc.

FIG 4 Detailed Map of the products being traded in the Triangle Trade. Public domain image.

fragile thing, a flawed human idea on paper. What *is* a country, a nation? A concept only recently conceived. Here, forced into existence through colonial devastation that, like that vengeful God, disrupts and displaces, erases and feeds difference. English and French will be the official languages, not Anishinaabemowin, Algonquin, Iroquoian, Inuktitut, Cree, nor the complex articulations of numerous displaced settlers, no hybrids, no creoles…

These catastrophic impacts and extinctions, traces of movement and migrations—of rock, of species, of cultures, of climate, on an earth constantly shifting, a terrain in continuous flux, slowly raked by glaciers—define this place currently called Canada. So many erratics placed with apparent precision and forethought, such clear markings. *Erratic* comes from the Latin "to wander," and how they wander, peoples displaced through colonization, the many who have become uncomfortable settlers, whose place is constantly being shaped by the dominant settler/colonizer obsessions over the symbols of home and belonging. Indigenous people know where they belong, while settlers struggle for belonging out of guilt or ignorance, or at worst through willful erasure; like the child protagonists in Wes Anderson's *Moonrise Kingdom,* shouting "THIS IS *OUR* LAND!"[4] into the wind, at the waves, into the elements. And all those who have landed here against their will or desire—through the forced migrations of slavery, conflict, and political turmoil, or the growing momentum of environmental disaster—have so many stories to tell: threads of living memory about this place, of endless movement, of beings out of space and time.

The dominant settler narrative, with its primary roots in the colonial empire of Britain, speaks of a landscape imagined as empty terrain, free of culture and history, to be mined and harvested for its resources: animal, vegetable, mineral; beaver, pine, copper; bison, wheat, oil; cod, oak, coal. *The* painters, the seven and their peers (so many of their agents remain, must I mention their names again?) reinforce this, deeply inscribe this, and out of their fantasy come maple leaves on Olympic mittens, on the jerseys of sports teams, on Mike Pearson's flag, and on the souvenir bottles of syrup and ice wine. If the land, the ground beneath our feet, truly defines Canada, then I'll follow threads out from the geological not to craft a science lecture, but to tell a tale. A tall tale? Perhaps. I am dreaming out from the stories I've inherited, to learn from what lies beneath, from all that lies embedded in rock that is far from empty or without memories.

Pangaea rips apart. A land mass—the Central Pangean Mountains, bedrock of what will become the Appalachians of eastern North America—is pushed apart by the birth of the Atlantic Ocean, dispersing sections into what will become Newfoundland, Iceland, Britain, and down through Europe to the West African coast (Figure 3, left). One day it will be reconnected through blood and suffering, through commerce and religion, cruel dominance and indifference; the Triangle Trade, anchored by the Middle Passage, bodies stolen and scattered, languages and customs systematically erased, cast aside, only to linger and haunt this place. Follow the paths of bodies and matter, guns and iron, from Britain to the "Slave Coast" of West Africa. Enslaved Africans cross the Middle Passage to Brazil and the Caribbean, then north with sugar and molasses, into colonial British North America (including Montreal, Quebec, Halifax, and such United Empire Loyalist strongholds in Upper Canada as Amherstburg, Queenston, and York); the foundational trade that anchors the development of the economy and continues to determine class and race divisions (Figure 4, left).

If you layer these maps—the underlying landforms pushed apart by the spreading Atlantic Ocean along the Mid-Atlantic Ridge, aligned with the Triangle Trade—the Appalachians mark the western boundary of the original British Colonies (so defined by King George III in the Royal Proclamation of 1763), and the rest continues through much of Britain and West Africa, with hints in the Caribbean and northeastern Brazil. A very different narrative of nation is defined by the soil beneath our feet, a deeply scarred terrain. To identify so deeply as a nation with this land means going much deeper than 150 years; deeper into the forces, geological and cultural, that shaped this space.

In the blink of an eye, the earth has rotated and the sun's gaze rakes over northern Quebec once more. Manicouagan blinks; the glint of reflected sunlight signals to the heavens. The forces that shaped and defined this circular lake and the flooding of the land for power in the 1970s—bringing this ancient trace of an interstellar traveller back to the surface—have had lasting impact, rippling out, echoing the shock waves of the meteor's impact.

In 1971, following the construction of the Daniel-Johnson Dam, Hydro-Québec initiated its "Project of the Century"—the James Bay Hydroelectric Development Project—ignoring the rights of the Inuit and Cree who lived around James Bay and in northern Quebec. But on November 11, 1975, following protests, court battles, and negotiations, the Government of Quebec, the James Bay Energy Corporation, the James Bay Development Corporation, Hydro-Québec, the Grand Council of the Crees (of Quebec), the Northern Quebec Inuit Association, and the Government of Canada signed the James Bay and Northern Quebec Agreement. This agreement offered, for the first time in Canada, a written contract that explicitly presented the rights of Indigenous people. It was as if the floodwaters from that first dam had inadvertently awakened and empowered a presence lingering deep in the earth, revealing to the settler-colonial powers a resiliency that lives and remembers.

I remember the first time I realized that the escarpment that cut through and defined my hometown was the edge of an ancient sea, and that the strange shapes cast into the rocks along the beach across the harbour were the traces of Ordovician brachiopods from 400 million years out (fern-like water plants whose stems resemble sections of esophagus). And when I climb up the hill from that beach to the Burlington Heights (a British Military designation from the War of 1812), I am scaling the Iroquois Bar, the edge of the Ice Age lake for which it is named. The old Hamilton Cemetery atop the bar is anchored by the remains of earthworks constructed by British troops who would advance east from here to meet the American forces at Stoney Creek. I weave my way through the mounds of earth, past gravestones carved to look like tree stumps, over the height of land to descend towards Cootes Paradise and Princess Point, where the Chonnonton Onguiaahra (Neutral people)[5] once harvested wild rice. I encounter a pair of tiny US flags, thin stars and stripes, fluttering in the winter wind at the base of a white stone monument.

Colonel William Winer Cooke, how strange to find him here; an officer in the United States Army during the American Civil War and the Black Hills War, he was George Armstrong Custer's right-hand man. Along with Custer, he led the massacre at Wounded Knee and then was subsequently sought out, killed, and ritually mutilated in righteous revenge by unknown Sioux warriors at the Battle of the Little Big Horn.[6] Winer Cooke was an erratic and destructive wanderer who landed here, now memorialized in a precarious symbol of Victorian mourning supported by a substrate of glacial till that regularly collapses and spills out onto the adjacent highway. I tear the flags from the ground and toss them into the nearby bin. One need not remember or honour this man here; not here, not now.

I remember the first time I realized that the Mohawk Trail School—my grade school that fronted onto Mohawk Road—was an homage to a people still living only a fifteen-minute drive south along the Grand River. The Six Nations of the Grand River, established by the Haudenosaunee Confederacy, were driven from their homeland in upstate New York after the American Revolution. They were led north by the Mohawk war chief Thayendanegea Joseph Brant out of the United States of America, a new nation founded on the disregard for historic treaties between settlers and the Indigenous peoples.

And I remember the first time I heard of the African Methodist community that had settled in the 1800s on the edge of the mountain brow, on the lip of the escarpment, at the shore of that ancient sea. I came to understand the depth of Black history in my hometown of Hamilton and throughout southwestern Ontario, and became aware that Black people and communities—framed and defined as immigrants and new Canadians—had been here for generations. They were here long before my grandparents came from Scotland and the north of England in the 1920s, after the Great War, escaping a collapsed economy.

Members of the Black community had fled slavery in the United States, only to return after the American Civil War because of the virulent racism they encountered in the new Canada. I didn't learn this in school. I learned this from artists but not from the art institutions that are implicated in this erasure and overwriting. This is a country that still assumes a person of colour is a newcomer, a country where the same stories are repeated, like the Alzheimer sufferer who takes comfort in endless repetition of the past and can't form new memories. The Canadian narrative

FIG 5 Springwater Meteorite Fragment, Royal Ontario Museum, M56008. With permission of the Royal Ontario Museum © ROM.

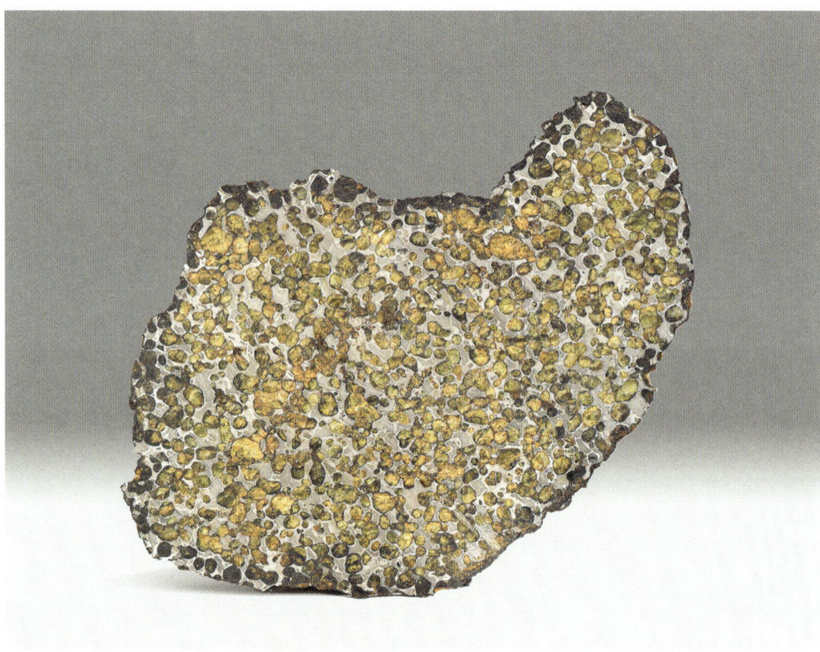

FIG 6 James Peters, *Louis Riel, a prisoner, in the camp of Major-General F.D. Middleton at Batoche, May 16, 1885*. Courtesy of Library and Archives Canada, MIKAN ID 3623590.

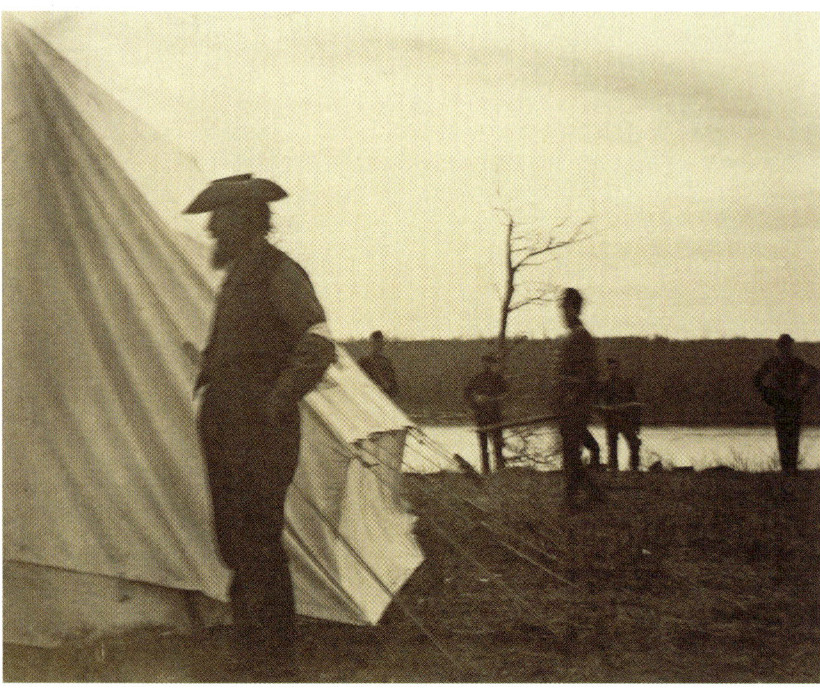

is dominated by amnesia and effacement. So many long-established communities have been ignored, consistently written out, and we all are poorer for this absence. The erasure imposed on living cultures reinforces the inauthenticity of the ruling narrative and results in deep trauma; this has meant the loss of language, family, memory. Yet cultures persist in their own time and space, not seeking validation in the flawed nationalism of a community that sees itself as dominant.

The jagged grey-green rock I hold is heavy. It speaks of a solidified liquid flow now shattered: a shatter cone. This one has a rich, dark patch where the oil from many hands has been rubbed into its porous surface. Such rocks were formed from the impact of a meteorite; catastrophic impacts liquefied the earth through intense heat and energy, then splashed and scattered material to and beyond the outer edges of the astrobleme. The second largest astrobleme on earth is in Sudbury (Sudbury is actually *in* the astrobleme), smaller than Chicxulub in Mexico and bigger than South Africa's Vredefort Crater. Debris from the Sudbury impact likely spread around the globe, to be eroded and absorbed as the earth continuously recycles itself. At its heart, magma consisting primarily of nickel, copper, platinum, palladium, and gold filled the crater and solidified. The contents of this crater were "discovered" in 1856 by settlers when the railway was being constructed to link the provinces, to unify this nation, built by migrant workers, many of whom would not be offered citizenship in the new Canada. The astrobleme is the foundation of modern Sudbury, the mineral structure that drew the extraction industry and its labourers—and, like other sites across northern Ontario, including the uranium mines in Elliot Lake—displaced the Anishinaabeg and contaminated their traditional territories.

The shatter cone I caress is from Sudbury, from the edge of an impact crater formed by an object (or being) approximately 10 to 15 kilometres in diameter, 1.8 to 1.9 billion years away (Figure 5). This object/being embedded itself and created a basin shaped like a nest, 62 by 30 kilometres and 15 kilometres deep; once round, the basin has been stretched to ovoid through time.

Standing in Copper Cliff, a claustrophobic web of narrow streets winding around self-built workers housing, and the first mine site in the heart of Greater Sudbury, one is towered over by the Super Stack—a structure that projects and disperses its toxic exhaust into the atmosphere, reaching distant communities. Copper is understood to be the congealed blood from the endless battles between the *animikiig* thunderbirds and *mishibizhiig* underwater panthers, between the sky world and the water world. Artist Michael Belmore tells me copper is found in its purest form here, and could be worked by the Anishinaabe without smelting technology, without pollution or contamination. It is considered to be a sacred material that now, stretched as fine wire and worked into thin coatings and film, underlies our current technological communication revolution. Copper is rewiring our brains and challenging the archaic notions of nation-states with defined borders. Thinking back to that impact nearly two billion years out, who is this meteorite, this object/being, that remains transformed in the earth, and lies buried and active in the ground?

From the top of the hill at Copper Cliff, one is not far from the opening of an active mine that also houses the SNOLAB. Located in one of Vale Limited's mine branch tunnels two kilometres below the surface, SNOLAB experiments include the search for supernova neutrinos and dark matter. The physicists at SNOLAB will tell you that only 4.9% of the universe consists of matter that can be "encountered or experienced,"[7] and the remaining 95.1% is comprised of 26.8% dark matter (an unidentified type of matter) and 68.3% dark energy (an unknown form of energy). These physicists have gone deep beneath the surface to wait; staring into deep time, looking into the Big Bang, speculating, hypothesizing, interpreting the sky world...

"4.6 billion years old," Ian Nicklin of the Royal Ontario Museum tells me, "from the beginning of the universe."[8] The object in my hands has been sliced off the larger pallasite, a stony-iron meteorite that looks like a giant charred potato. Its outer surface appears dark and rusted (Figure 5, left). Within, it consists of the mineral olivine and the nickel/iron alloy kamacite. Sliced and polished, it reveals a constellation of amber-coloured mineral fragments enmeshed in heavy silver metal. It seems to hum with energy, as if you are holding the birth of the universe. This is the Springwater meteorite, found in Springwater, Saskatchewan, in 1931.

Located at 51° 58′ N, 108° 22′ W, Springwater is now a virtual ghost town, in the heart of the Rural Municipality of Biggar 347, with a population density of 0.5 people per square kilometre. An hour west of Saskatoon, it is two hours from Batoche, where, in May of 1885, Louis Riel, Poundmaker, and Big Bear, with their Métis and Cree fighters, made a final stand. The Canadian army would eventually prevail, ending the provisional government and Riel's dreams of an independent state. Refusing to grant clemency to Riel, who was sentenced to death by hanging for treason, Prime Minister Sir John A. Macdonald blustered, "He shall die though every dog in Quebec bark in his favour."[9] Macdonald, Canada's first prime minister in 1867, would go on to establish the Indian Act, declaring, "The great aim of our legislation has been to do away with the tribal system and assimilate the Indian people in all respects with the other inhabitants of the Dominion as speedily as they are fit to change."[10] Macdonald was committed to establishing Canada through the erasure of Indigenous peoples—the foundation of Canada 150.

Riel, a visionary, saw beyond this. "Deeds are not accomplished in a few days, or in a few hours," he once said. "A century is only a spoke in the wheel of everlasting time."[11]

Here is a haunting image of Riel following his capture at Batoche (Figure 6, left). He's standing silhouetted against a white tent, hands in pockets, with a rumpled hat and a distinct scruffy beard. He looks thin, not the robust, broad-chested figure often described. He appears to be staring hard at his tent, its billowing white fabric rippling and folding, rising up to a sharp peak just beyond the top-left corner of the frame. Riel seems to be contemplating his next move, his next transcendent journey in time, endless, motionless, against this bright white peak that is strangely reminiscent of Lawren S. Harris's distorted icon, *Mt. Lefroy*.

Shuvinai Ashoona and I stand fixated on the sharply delineated, white Arctic peaks of another Lawren Harris canvas. "Where are all the people?" she wonders aloud. "Where are the animals?" She goes on to describe the giant monster fish that she imagines lingers beneath the waves. "The mountains are Inuktitut," she tells me, "they are my language. They go down into the earth, into the ground, to meet the dead." She smiles and shrugs and turns away from the painting. "Why can't they see that?" she whispers.[12] *Why can't we see that?*

Andrew Hunter is a curator, artist, writer, educator, and community researcher. Since 2013, he has been the Fredrik S. Eaton Curator, Canadian Art, at the Art Gallery of Ontario. He lives in Hamilton.

NOTES

1. According to the *Commission de toponymie du Québec*.

2. Ibid.

3. There are many sources for this translation, with Nakuk Pech's *The Chronicle of Chac Xulub Chen* (1562) being the primary source most commonly cited.

4. Wes Anderson and Roman Coppola, *Moonrise Kingdom,* directed by Wes Anderson (Indian Paintbrush, American Empirical Pictures, 2012).

5. The Neutral Nation was an Iroquoian-speaking people whose traditional territory was located along the north shores of Lake Ontario and Lake Erie. The Iroquois Confederacy largely wiped out the Neutral Nation in the mid-17th century during the Beaver Wars, and surviving Neutrals were absorbed into other nations.

6. "Cooke...was scalped twice—the second scalp being one of his prodigiously long flowing side-whiskers..." Evan S. Connell, *Son of the Morning Star: Custer and Little Bighorn* (New York: MacMillan, 1984). Descriptions of Cooke's demise are recorded in numerous Sioux accounts of the battle, including a hand-painted buffalo hide winter count in the collection of the Autry Museum of the American West, Los Angeles.

7. From a conversation between the author and physicists at SNOLAB, October 2012.

8. In conversation with the author, August 2016.

9. Claude Bélanger, "North-West Rebellion—Canadian History" *L'Encyclopédie de l'histoire du Québec/The Quebec History Encyclopedia* (Westmount: Marianopolis College, 2007).

10. Sir John A. Macdonald, Superintendent General of Indian Affairs, "Sessional Papers," *Memorandum to Privy Council*, Volume 16, January 3, 1887, in Blaire Stonechild, *The New Buffalo: The Struggle for Aboriginal Post-Secondary Education* (Winnipeg: University of Manitoba Press, 2006), 37.

11. *The Montreal Weekly Star* (August 22, 1885), in *War in the West: Voices of the 1885 Rebellion,* eds. Rudy Henry Wiebe and Bob Beal (Toronto: McClelland and Stewart, 1985), 2.

12. Artist Shuvinai Ashoona of Kinngait/Cape Dorset, Baffin Island, Nunavut, in conversation with the author, March 2017.

Finding Home

Notes on Inclusion and Hospitality in Art Institutions in Canada

Srimoyee Mitra

I had an amazing experience last year: I gave birth. It was an out-of-body experience. As I rushed to the hospital for an emergency C-section, I thought of my mother and grandmothers and the matrix of ideas, experiences, and histories that link us. I imagined maternal matrices as intergenerational spaces and places of arrival and becoming. I realized that the womb's ability to *welcome*—into my body, my home—bridges boundaries of self and other, private and public, domestic and foreign.[1] Could such an expansive matrix of hospitality be extended beyond the home?[2]

The notion of home has always been an emotionally charged space for me, functioning as a space of confinement as well as an inexhaustible reservoir of knowledge and energy on which to build and expand.[3] I grew up in a loving and supportive middle-class family almost four decades after the Partition of colonial India, which coincided with its Independence in 1947. My parents were the first generation of citizens born at a time when the successful national independence struggle gave birth to a democratic socialist nation-state. They nurtured and reiterated the values of democracy, secularism, and "unity in diversity"—the founding principles of the Indian constitution.

My grandmother's tales of the freedom movement made a lasting impression on me as a young girl. She participated in the struggle as an actor and singer concerned with the development of independent Bengali literature and the arts, and as one of the founding members of the Indian People's Theatre Association in Kolkata. She was also an activist canvassing door to door for the left, asking women to join the Independence struggle, all the while dodging the British colonial police. Her deeply personal experience and radical anecdotes informed my understanding of women's roles in the birth of the nation.[4] Many years later, I learned that the birth of India as a free nation was also the scene of unprecedented collective violence. Awareness of the intergenerational trauma that emerged from the horrific brutality on both sides of the border—including mass abductions and rape—radically shaped my worldview, and informs a sense of urgency in my work.

At the age of eighteen, I moved to Canada as an international student. Here, I am categorized as South Asian, rather than as an Indian person raised in Mumbai. As such, the specificity of my cultural heritage is reduced to a statistic in Canada, lumped in with the highly diverse identities of the Indian subcontinent, known as South Asia in the West.[5] The effacement of different temporal and spatial registers of migrants and refugees perpetuates assimilationist "song-and-sari multiculturalism,"[6] while expanding the legacy of settler colonialism. Many people from India migrated to Canada in the late nineteenth and early twentieth centuries as British colonial subjects, well before India, Pakistan, and Bangladesh were independent nations. Most folks came as indentured labourers, and they bore the consequences of cultural and intergenerational loss, fragmentation, and marginalization in a fundamentally racist and colonial society.

I have learned that "Indian" is a loaded term in Canada. It is deeply linked to heinous crimes committed by the colonial regimes to disenfranchise and alienate First Nations, Métis, and Inuit peoples, with the establishment of the Indian residential schools in 1860 and the Indian Act in 1876. The systemic socio-economic barriers and intergenerational loss of Indigenous cultures, communities, and identities are still pervasive within contemporary Canadian society. Thus there are parallels between the divergent experiences of "Indian-ness" experienced by Indigenous and so-called South Asian peoples in Canada.

I have lived in Canada for fifteen years now. I have grown tremendously and learned many life lessons; some were painful and traumatic, yet many have been joyous and empowering. The far-reaching tentacles of the imperialist project that continue to divide and marginalize racialized and Indigenous communities in different parts of the world, including Canada, has transformed my subjectivity. The objective and impetus of my life's work has shifted from a post-colonial discourse of displacement and migration to an analysis of the colonial, systemic barriers that are embedded in the infrastructure and institutions in which I live and work. This involves confronting the dilemma of perpetuating the settler legacy as a recent migrant in Canada, where the immigration policy was established by European settlers and played a crucial role in mobilizing colonialism in Canada throughout the nineteenth and twentieth centuries. (Likewise, the point-based immigration system in the twenty-first century in Canada is built on neo-liberal and neo-colonial assumptions of race and identity, which have a major influence on contemporary Canadian narratives of culture and history.) By retracing my genealogy, I unlearn and unsettle my scripted role as a migrant-settler in everyday life. As a curator, I consistently attempt to build decolonial and caring dialogue with artists, artworks, and general audiences, based on mutual respect.[7]

In Sara Ahmed's *On Being Included,* she writes that to account for racism is to offer a different account of the world. She explains this as the "stranger experience," where certain bodies become more noticeable, and do not pass through without being stopped or being held up.[8] While Ahmed's research is located within academic institutions, she raises important questions on diversity and equality that are timely and relevant for art organizations, public galleries, and museums in Canada. She discusses the complexities of being held responsible for fostering diversity and equality as people of colour functioning within Eurocentric institutions. These responsibilities are often unevenly distributed, and the distribution itself is political.[9] By the same token, in Canadian public galleries and museums, a large percentage of programmers/curators working on projects that explore questions of social justice, race, and equity are people of colour. Moreover, the expectation is often that a programmer of colour will take on the responsibility for developing "culturally diverse" (code for non-Euro-American) programming. In this way, many art institutions simply offload the responsibility to implement strategies of inclusion onto employees of colour rather than by making systemic changes. This not only undermines the efficacy and reach of the programs but also maintains the dominant settler definitions of Canadian culture.

I experienced such ghettoization first-hand in graduate school, while pursuing a master's in art history. I was consistently encouraged by friends and faculty to intern at SAVAC (South Asian Visual Arts Centre) more than any other arts institution in Toronto, while my peers were encouraged to explore internships at places like the Power Plant, AGYU,

Gallery 44, and so on. While I appreciated their enthusiasm, it was clear that neither SAVAC nor I fell into the normative view of "Canadian" art. I ended up interning for SAVAC and stayed on for three years. Every year, we received requests and invitations from regional galleries to partner with us. In this way, the galleries filled their "cultural diversity" quota before their operating grants were due. We would consider each request very carefully before accepting the invitation—there is a fine line between tokenism and representation.

My experience at SAVAC taught me that meaningful collaborations always involve honest dialogue that may confront entrenched biases and value systems. The act of working with another individual or group towards a common goal entails active listening, deep thinking, and mutual respect. Art has an incredible capacity to unpack and reckon with difficult, divisive issues in ways that are intuitive, multi-sensorial, and emotional. For me, this exercise of finding common ground (with another peer/artist/filmmaker/designer/architect/arts institution) lies at the core of my practice and love of curating. It is a way of working that is inherently process-based, dialogic, and empathy-building, while rupturing the consistent threat of ghettoization. Every exhibition/project/performance demands that we rethink and renew questions of place and space, arrival, and belonging. It enables ideas and experiences to flow and interact in the gallery space. Audiences can experience and immerse themselves in multiple world views, anecdotes, and critiques that are different from their own. Could such an expansive matrix of hospitality be extended beyond the gallery?[10]

Canada's 150th birthday is a critical platform for fearless introspection and for the re-invention of ideas of nationhood, citizenship, and belonging. As cultural workers, we must take the lead to engage in courageous, painful dialogues to uproot the entrenched colonial legacy and value systems that many art museums and public galleries in Canada perpetuate. Such fearlessness emerges from intergenerational and interstitial knowledge systems that are embedded in the untold stories of triumph and change-making within Indigenous, migrant, refugee, and Black communities, whose voices continue to be silenced and marginalized. Acknowledging our ongoing contributions, and unlearning the culture of settling in ways that divide people along socio-economic, linguistic, cultural, and racial lines, will lay the foundations for a burgeoning framework of decolonization. I imagine a framework "that accounts for the treatment of others with limitless attention and expectation;" one that "entails an active gesture of welcoming, greeting, sheltering, and in many cases nourishing."[11] I imagine such expansive acts of hospitality transforming oppressive social, political, and cultural barriers, and making space for the inclusion of vibrant and robust vernacular perspectives through Indigenous, migrant, refugee, and Black lenses.

Much to my wonder and amazement, when a little crying, delicate baby with blood-smothered skin emerged from within me, I imagined citizenship as kinship, and home and belonging as friendship-building—as learning "to become fluent in each other's histories."[12] The womb's capacity to welcome bridges conventional boundaries. Through working at public galleries and artist-run centres, I realized that the gallery space embodies a womb-like quality that can function as a gestational space, an active and changing space that welcomes and generates artworks, public programs, and publications. I see my role as a curator and cultural worker as deeply linked to the maternal matrices where intergenerational ideas, experiences, and histories of art, aesthetics, culture, and design are in constant states of flux and becoming.

Srimoyee Mitra is the director of the Stamps Art Gallery at The Penny W. Stamps School of Art & Design, University of Michigan (Ann Arbor). Previously, she was the curator of contemporary Art at the Art Gallery of Windsor, where she curated the Border Cultures *series.*

NOTES

1. Irina Aristarkhova, *The Hospitality Matrix* (New York: Columbia University Press, 2012), 4.

2. Ibid., 16.

3. Trinh T. Minh-ha, *Elsewhere, within Here* (New York: Rutledge, 2011), 34.

4. Srimoyee Mitra, "Sensing Borders," in *Border Cultures,* ed. Srimoyee Mitra (London: Black Dog Publishing, 2015), 10.

5. Chandra Talpade Mohanty, *Feminism without Borders* (New York and Durham, NC: Duke University Press, 2003), 47.

6. Jason Kenney, "Speaking Notes for the Honourable Jason Kenney, P.C., M.P. Minister of Citizenship, Immigration and Multiculturalism, 'Good Citizenship: The Duty to Integrate' at Huron University College's Canadian Leaders Speakers' Series," Immigration Refugees and Citizenship Canada, posted March 18, 2009.

7. Mitra, "Sensing Borders," 15.

8. Sara Ahmed, *On Being Included* (Durham, NC and London: Duke University Press, 2012), 4.

9. Ibid., 5.

10. Aristarkhova, *The Hospitality Matrix,* 16.

11. Ibid., 45.

12. Mohanty, *Feminism without Borders,* 125.

Ready?

Rachelle Dickenson

When Andrew Hunter asked me to contribute my perspective on Canada 150, I was honoured. My initial response to the topic was contradictory—I laughed out loud and then abruptly stopped, filled with doubt. Like many people, I can't help but see this anniversary as a celebration of colonization.[1]

As a woman with Métis ancestry raised settler,[2] I've spent much of my adult life learning about Indigenous and Canadian art histories and colonialism. I have had the privilege to learn from, work, and hang out with Indigenous and ally artists, curators, and scholars. I have also experienced the denial and/or strategic displacement of histories of oppression and violence in Canadian cultural institutions.

I continue to learn—as a student, instructor, or curator in institutions such as art galleries and universities—about long-repressed histories of Indigenous resistance and resurgence within political and diplomatic negotiations and cultural activisms over the last five hundred years. These expressions are often gathered together by cultural practitioners in resistance to, or in collaboration with, colonial celebrations such as Expo 67 in Montreal and the 125th celebration of Canadian confederation in 1992. Such celebrations of Canada have inspired a dynamic range of transformative expressions of Indigenous sovereignty.[3]

So, when I came to my computer to write this perspective piece, the first thing I thought of was the determination of Indigenous peoples to "not only survive but, in many ways, thrive" within the colonial structures of Canada.[4] This thought was followed by my recollection of a recording I'd heard of George Erasmus's impassioned reproach given during a 125th anniversary planning conference in Ottawa in 1989. What resonated particularly for me was his voice—raw with anger, it rang in my ears, and rang true in this moment as much as it did in the late 1980s:

> What are we gonna do about the next 500 years!... I don't think that we have a solitary thing that we should be celebrating about, unless we are going to do something different in the future. It's really time for some change. It's really time that the European people, and their descendants, and the rest that are here, that are now Canadians, seriously begin to address the basic relationship they have with this land and the people that were here first.[5]

This speech was reprinted in *Indigena: Contemporary Native Perspectives in Canadian Art*, an exhibition catalogue produced for the Canadian Museum of Civilization in 1992 to mark the 125th anniversary of confederation. *Indigena*, co-curated by Lee-Ann Martin and Gerald McMaster, brought together responses from Indigenous artists and writers as an intervention opposing the celebration of confederation and hundreds of years of colonization, "celebrating [instead] both diversity and cultural tenacity."[6]

While sitting at my desk in 2017—listening to Erasmus's words and reading them reproduced in *Indigena*, recalling vivid images of The Indians of Canada Pavilion at Expo 67, and reflecting on Canada 150—I am awash with contradictory feelings. What resounds above all are the ways that art makes evident both Indigenous resilience and Canadian colonial processes by excavating repressed histories, restoring accurate representations of Indigenous/settler encounters, and uncovering genocidal and assimilationist government policies and practices.

The Indians of Canada Pavilion, for example, destroyed the notion of a resolved, settled, Canadian nation-state.[7] Likewise, exhibitions such as *Indigena*, *Every. Now. Then*, and many, many others, continue to challenge Canadian colonialism. These acts of resistance, on national and international stages, mark the slow erosion of Canadian national "fantasies of possession [and] entitlement."[8] The stories told by invaders, colonialists, settlers, and the state to legitimate the seizure of Indigenous lands ranged from outright lies to structural rationalizations. These stories were made manifest through the elimination of Indigenous peoples and territorial rights, by producing new laws, new histories, and new peoples, which continue to ensure settler access to, and control of, land and resources.[9]

Concurrently, Indigenous leaders, activists, scholars, artists, and curators have been revitalizing, revisioning, and activating Indigenous governance through expressions of sovereignty. Such initiatives in policy, economic, and artistic activisms contest the truth of settler sovereignty, uncover Indigenous/settler encounters of exchange and collaboration, and bring Indigenous territorial and political rights to the fore.

This Canada 150 moment is thunderous, the voices of artists, activists, scholars, and curators contesting colonialism across centuries, building legacies of cultural activism and resistance. I return to Erasmus in agreement: we don't have anything to celebrate unless "Canadians seriously begin to address the basic relationship they have with this land and the people that were here first." First Nations, Métis, and Inuit peoples have much to honour—thousands of years of living on this land, creating art, building nations, carrying traditions through innovation and incredible tenacity. The question remains, is Canada ready to join in celebrating this?

Rachelle Dickenson is an independent curator and Ph.D. student at Carleton University. She was formerly curatorial assistant in the Indigenous Art Department at the National Gallery of Canada and has an M.A. in Art History from McGill University. She lives in Ottawa.

The author would like to thank Andrew Hunter, Dr. Eva Mackey, Steven Loft, Dr. Carla Taunton, Barry Ace, and Judy Lovell for their support and feedback.

NOTES

1. Nadya Kwandibens, Anishinaabe/Ojibwe photographer living in Toronto: "The way I see it is, these celebrations are a celebration of colonialism and, as an Indigenous person, I'm choosing not to celebrate colonialism," in Deana Sumanac-Johnson, "Telling their stories or opting out: Indigenous artists on Canada 150," *CBC News*, February 7, 2017 (available online). Alicia Elliott, "#Resistance150: Christi Belcourt on Indigenous history, resilience and resurgence," *CBC Canada150*, February 22, 2017 (available online). See also #Colonization150.

2. "Settler" is a much-debated term often used to describe non-Indigenous persons with ancestry that is linked to historical and/or contemporary colonial processes, through settlement on Indigenous lands and immigration. There is much important discussion about the particularities of the term in Canadian and US contexts. Eva Mackey, *House of Difference: Cultural Politics and National Identity in Canada* (Toronto: University of Toronto Press, 1999); and *Unsettled Expectations: Uncertainty, Land and Settler Decolonization* (Halifax and Winnipeg: Fernwood Publishing, 2016). Patrick Wolfe, "Settler Colonialism and the Elimination of the Native," *Journal of Genocide Research* 8, no. 4 (2006): 387–409. Mark Rifkin, "Settler Common Sense," *Settler Colonial Studies* 3, no. 3–4 (2013): 322–40.

3. Scholars such as Jolene Rickard (Tuscarora) and Michelle Raheja consider the development of Indigenous sovereignty as an appropriation of the European concept of sovereignty. However, through analysis of Indigenous art, film, and curatorial practices, they argue that the term has diversified beyond the Euro-Western application to encompass nation-specific and land-based Indigenous world views. In the work of these scholars and others, like Steven Loft, conceptualizations of Indigenous sovereignty are aggregated through art making to assert Indigenous self-determination in contemporary North American colonial contexts. In other words, many (but not all) Indigenous scholars, artists, and curators have appropriated and expanded the Euro-Western concept of sovereignty to both re-emphasize the nation-to-nation relationships established through treaty making during settlement, and to assert the legitimacy of Indigenous self-governance in today's arts-based, socio-economic political contexts. Jolene Rickard, "Visualizing Sovereignty in the Time of Biometric Sensors," *South Atlantic Quarterly* 110, no. 2 (2011): 467; and "Sovereignty: A Line in the Sand," *Aperture* no. 139, Spring (1995): 51–54. Michelle H. Raheja, "Reading Nanook's Smile: Visual Sovereignty, Indigenous Revisions of Ethnography, and Atanarjuat (The Fast Runner)," *American Quarterly* 59, no. 4 (2007): 1159–85. Steven Loft, "Sovereignty, Subjectivity and Social Action: The Films of Alanis Obomsawin," in *Transference, Tradition, Technology: Native New Media Exploring Visual and Digital Culture* (Banff: Walter Phillips Gallery, 2005), 60–67.

4. Barry Ace, in a phone conversation with the author, March 8, 2017. Thank you to Barry, who helped me focus this discussion, and work through the frustration that comes with the ubiquitous assertions of settler sovereignty in these types of celebrations.

5. Georges Erasmus, "Georges Erasmus: Nothing to celebrate," *CBC Morningside,* broadcast October 16, 1989 (digital archive available online).

6. Gerald McMaster and Lee-Ann Martin, eds., *Indigena: Contemporary Native Perspectives in Canadian Art* (Vancouver: Douglas & McIntyre, 1992).

7. Tuck and Yang argue that the aspiration towards a settled nation-state, wherein colonization is complete, is another "settler move to innocence." Eve Tuck and K. Wayne Yang, "Decolonization Is Not a Metaphor," *Decolonization: Indigeneity, Education and Society* 1, no. 1 (2012): 1–40.

8. Eva Mackey refers to such narratives as "the elaborate and illogical (though extensively rationalized) 'fantasies of possession' and 'fantasies of entitlement' that have built settler certainty," through the construction of settler sovereignty. Eva Mackey, *Unsettled Expectations: Uncertainty, Land and Settler Decolonization* (Halifax and Winnipeg: Fernwood Publishing, 2016), 10. Eve Tuck and K. Wayne Yang also articulate "fantasies" of settler sovereignty as strategies to secure settler sovereignty, or what they call "settler moves to innocence," in "Decolonization Is Not a Metaphor."

9. Patrick Wolfe, "Settler Colonialism and the Elimination of the Native," *Journal of Genocide Research* 8, no. 4 (2006): 387–409.

Inclusions and Omissions
Imaginings of Canadian Nation-ness

Rosie Spooner

Having grown up in downtown Toronto but spent most of my adult years in Glasgow, I am looking at Canada 150 with an eye for how the country is presenting itself to those outwith its borders. I find myself interrogating attempts at synopsizing Canada, which tend to abridge 150 years of history and simultaneously stake a claim to the country's future. I am especially interested in how current understandings of Canada compare to those that prevailed during the period when the country was ostensibly in its infancy. As a cultural historian, I see this as an opportune moment to explore the role that visual and material practices play in constructing imaginings and projections of Canadian nationhood, and reflect on how such visions have shifted and evolved. What symbols have been used to encapsulate a sense of nation-ness? What experiences and subjectivities are included within national iconographies, and conversely, which are left out?

At the time of Confederation, world's fairs and international exhibitions were key sites at which national interests were negotiated and national identities were promoted. Executed on a phenomenal scale, these spectacles were held all over the world, although principally in large European and North American cities like London, Paris, and New York. Presenting art, design, and industrial culture in elaborate and fanciful ways, they routinely enticed spectators in the millions. Canada was a regular contributor to overseas exhibitions, organizing displays that were dominated by natural resources (Figure 1). Somewhat surprisingly, things as inert as grain samples, mineral specimens, and preserved fruit often rivalled cutting-edge machinery and technology, as well as pageants, rides, and amusements, for the public's attention. This is because raw materials performed an important illustrative role at these events, with the types of objects consistently exhibited by the Canadian government fitting neatly within a larger cultural discourse. As a popular guide to London's Great Exhibition of 1851 explained to its Victorian readers, "the distance between the raw material and the perfected work is the measure of the conquest of man over the external world."[1]

While at first glance Canada's exhibits characterized the Dominion's natural resources and attendant wealth, they also served to insert the country into a global order of progress and civilization, albeit a decidedly Eurocentric one. The Canadian government strove to elevate the country's position in this hierarchy by stressing its role as a chief supplier of raw materials to Britain and the wider empire. This reveals that mapping, cultivating, and controlling the natural environment were fundamental traits of a nascent national identity. Viewed through this lens, Canada's exhaustive displays of rocks, grasses, and canned foods—all meticulously labelled to indicate their different properties, uses, and places of origin—take on deeply imaginative qualities. This has echoes of Northrop Frye's assertion that identity "is primarily a cultural and imaginative question," and so betrays the influence of creative instinct.[2]

According to the historian Phillip Buckner, "Canadians entered the twentieth century increasingly self-confident about their nation's future and determined to play a more important part in world affairs."[3] This was evident in the Canadian government's approach to world's fairs and international exhibitions, whereby these spectacles were used as platforms for dispelling dominant views held overseas, particularly in the so-called imperial "mother country." Authorities were especially keen to shed Canada's reputation as a rugged wilderness with a sparse population, a colonial construct rooted in notions of the picturesque that had been moulded by European visual and literary depictions (Figures 2 and 3). Indeed, renderings of the natural world presented by exploration and travel accounts were inherently distorted, offering "projections of European ideas, values, and tastes," rather than reflections of any material and social realities.[4]

Commentary in exhibition catalogues and the press suggest the government succeeded in its ambition, stimulating a revised understanding of what Canada was like, and changing popular opinions in Britain. As one exhibition guide noted, those "who have generally associated Canada with tobogganing, sleigh bells, and fur overcoats will no doubt be surprised at the immense variety of its fruits... [which] grow wild and luxuriantly."[5] Striving to do more than just dislodge existing conceptions of Canada, the government's displays at nineteenth and twentieth-century exhibitions were designed to promote an understanding of what made Canada distinct, in the hope of attracting British emigrants and investors. Its exhibits aimed to demonstrate that life in the Dominion was not typified by mere subsistence and survival in a constantly cold country, but that it could offer prosperity. It is worth underlining, however, that such desires for increased settlement and investment negated Indigenous interests. Additionally, such enticements were generally reserved for British audiences, and seldom extended to prospective migrants from what were then regarded as less desirable places, such as southern Europe, the Indian subcontinent, and Southeast Asia.

Whether preserved fruits or processed foodstuffs, extracted minerals or harvested grains, Massey-Harris wheat binders, or images of the Canadian Pacific Railway, the objects selected by the Canadian government for public display signified an ability to harness the land and its natural resources. A particularly potent symbol of this narrative appeared at the Glasgow International Exhibition of 1901. The vision of Canada presented here, one constructed chiefly by government agencies, was not just of an expansive, resource-rich landscape. It also portrayed

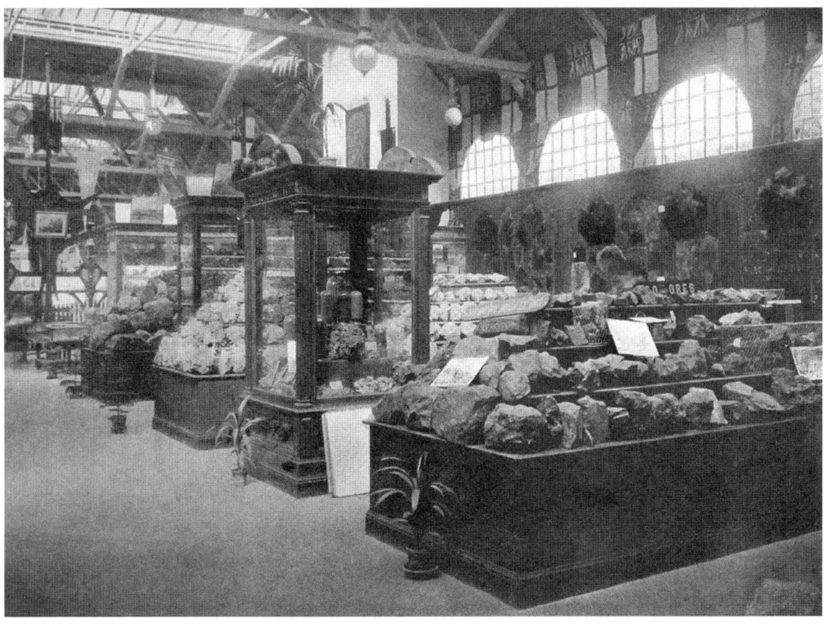

FIG 1 Mineral displays of the Canadian Court inside the Industrial Hall at the Glasgow International Exhibition of 1901. Photograph published in *The Exhibition Illustrated*, July 27, 1901. © CSG CIC Glasgow Museums and Libraries Collection: The Mitchell Library, Archives, LK5.2505.

key markers of a nation-state, a message that was a priority in light of the fact that Canada had become a federated country less than thirty-five years earlier. The form chosen to symbolize this nexus of ideas was something called an agricultural trophy—a large structure modelled in the shape of the spire atop the parliamentary library in Ottawa, the still relatively new national capital (Figure 4). This installation measured thirty-five feet high and sixty-five feet in circumference, and was made entirely out of agricultural produce drawn from across the country, such as corn, oats, barley, wheat, rye, and tobacco.

Fittingly, the agricultural trophy was designed by an employee of the Department of Agriculture's Experimental Farms unit named W.H. Hay, whose evocative description points to its function as a rhetorical tool that conveyed a distinct ideology:

> [T]he grain was massed and arranged in gothic arches and in circles, and when completed the structure had the appearance of an immense temple of cereals. Coats of arms of the provinces were placed over each of the main arches, and some fine specimens of mounted 'prairie chickens' were distributed among the sheaves of grain... Good views were shown of settlers' homes, giving the appearance of the farm when first located, and again a few years later under improved conditions... The agricultural trophy elicited the admiration of visitors on every hand for its colossal character.[6]

Hay's work was evidently intended to be an allegory for a cohesive national unit. Weaving together a singular vision of Canada—both metaphorically and materially—it exhibited a considered sense of nation-ness that superseded regional ties, and supplanted social and cultural plurality. Stitching over any fissures and fractures, it had no loose ends. This three-dimensional portrait of Canada from the turn of the last century revealed a settler-colonial society, an image of the nation that omitted the presence of many, and in particular negated the sovereignty of Indigenous peoples.

Reflecting on past moments when Canada sought to showcase itself to a wider world offers occasion to trace the lineage of ideas that remain central to imaginings of *Canadian-ness,* but which often overlook histories of conflict and contestation, particularly over issues of land and place, and attendant questions over who has access to these spaces and who belongs within them. Indeed, as Edward Said explains, "There is in all nationally defined cultures... an aspiration to sovereignty, to sway, and to dominance."[7] This is a timely reminder. The passage of the first British North America Act in 1867 brought together three existing colonies—the Province of Canada (now Ontario and Quebec), New Brunswick, and Nova Scotia—to create a new state called the Dominion of Canada. Although ostensibly self-governing, it would take another 115 years and twenty additional UK parliamentary acts for all legislative and constitutional powers to be transferred to Canadian authorities.

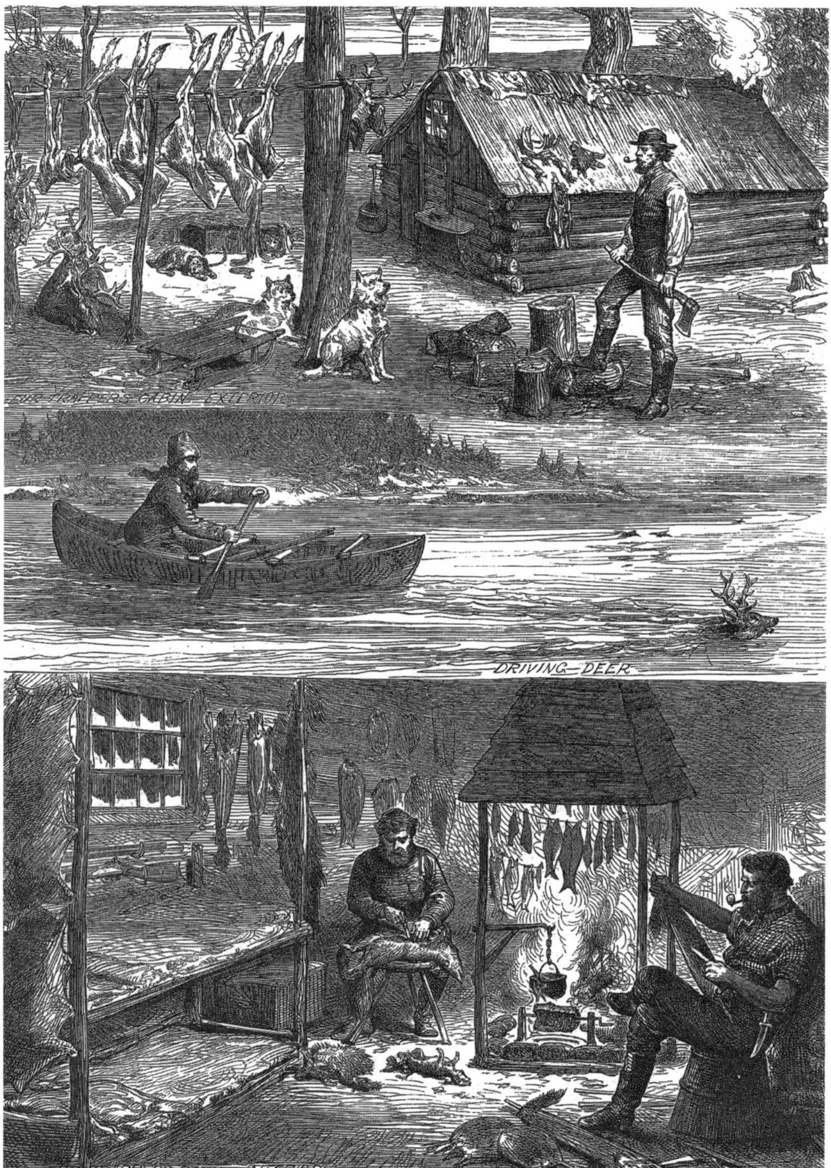

FIG 2 *Fur Trappers in the Backwoods of Canada.* Published in *Illustrated London News*, May 15, 1880. Collection of the author.

FIG 3 *Left*: The Doulton Fountain as it stood in front of the Main Building of the Glasgow International Exhibition of 1888. By permission of University of Glasgow Library, Special Collections, Sp.Coll. PhotoB4. *Right*: The Canadian figurative group on the Doulton Fountain as seen today. Photograph courtesy of Paul Twynam.

FIG 4 The Agricultural Trophy, the centrepiece of the Canadian Pavilion at the Glasgow International Exhibition of 1901. Photograph published in *The Exhibition Illustrated*, July 27, 1901. ©CSG CIC Glasgow Museums and Libraries Collection: The Mitchell Library, Archives, LK5.2505.

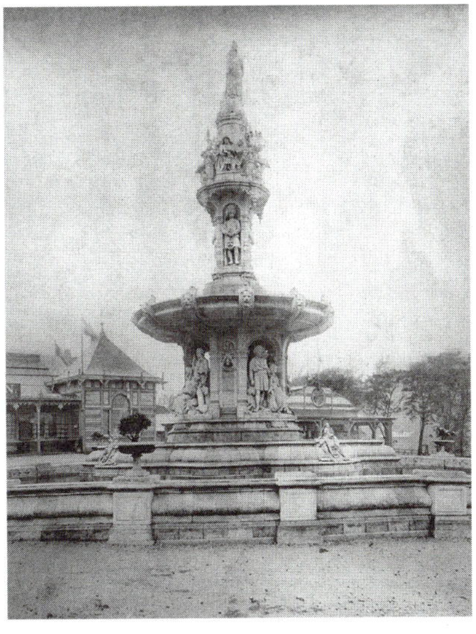

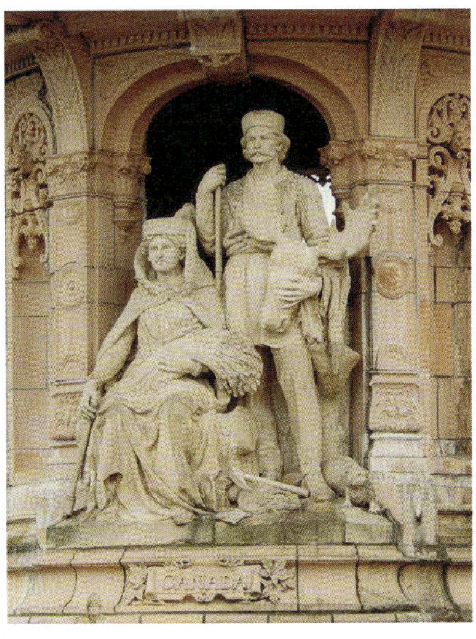

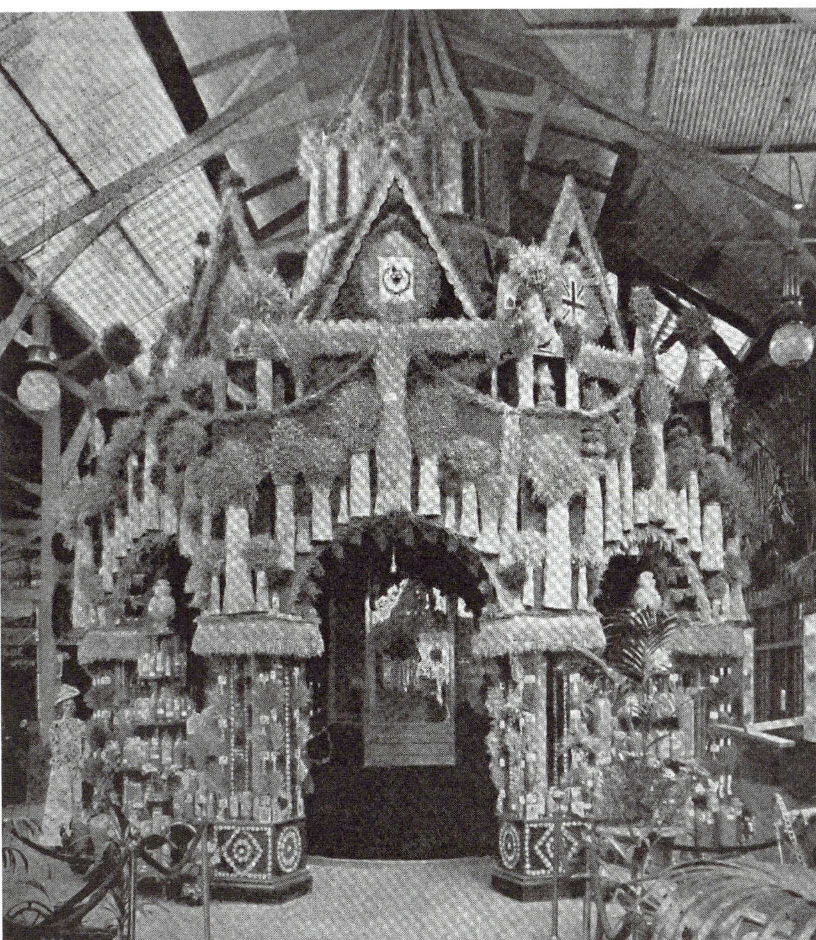

Perhaps of greater consequence, the physical shape and social composition of Canada changed dramatically over these years. Colonialist policies, for example, caused increased settlement at the expense of First Nations societies that inhabited, used, and acted as guardians of the land—which was purposefully territorialized by the nation-state and affiliated institutions. This silencing would seem to have found a parallel at world's fairs and international exhibitions, since Canada's displays overlooked this aspect of the country's burgeoning national story, focusing instead on the narrative that it was ripe with promise.

Canada 150 is a celebration of a nation on a national scale. Over the course of this year, well-rehearsed stories we tell each other as Canadians will be performed anew in the hope of shoring up a shared sense of belonging and nationhood. Viewing these gestures with skepticism and taking a critical approach, however, is crucial if reverting to historic constructions of national identity that bolster settler-colonial ambitions is to be avoided. Exhibitions like *Every. Now. Then: Reframing Nationhood* offer opportunities to examine how national iconographies have come into being, and judiciously reflect on the ways they are continually rehashed, reformulated, and rebuilt. This in turn allows us to further understand contemporary resonances that such myths of collective identity often obfuscate, and yet do not render wholly invisible.

Dr. Rosie Spooner is a researcher, writer, and educator, and is currently Lecturer in Design History and Theory at the Glasgow School of Art. She holds a Ph.D. in History of Art (University of Glasgow) and an M.A. in Colonial and Postcolonial Studies (University of Bristol). She lives in Glasgow.

NOTES

1. John Tallis and Jacob George Strutt, *History and Description of the Crystal Palace; and the Exhibition of the World's Industry in 1851; Illustrated by Beautiful Steel Engravings from Original Drawings and Daguerreotypes by Beard, Mayall, Etc.* (London: John Tallis & Co., 1852), 14.

2. Northrop Frye, *Bush Garden: Essays on the Canadian Imagination* (Toronto: University of Toronto Press, 1971), i.

3. Phillip Buckner, "The Creation of the Dominion of Canada, 1860–1901," in *Canada and the British Empire*, ed. Phillip Buckner (Oxford: Oxford University Press, 2008), 67.

4. Brian S. Osborne, "The Iconography of Nationhood in Canadian Art," in *The Iconography of Landscape: Essays on the Symbolic Representation, Design and Use of Past Environments*, eds. Denis Cosgrove and Stephen Daniels (Cambridge: Cambridge University Press, 1988), 163. See also Leanne Betasamosake Simpson, ed., *Lighting the Eighth Fire: The Liberation, Resurgence and Protection of Indigenous Nations* (Winnipeg: Arbeiter Ring Publishing, 2008); and Suzanne Zeller, *Inventing Canada: Early Victorian Science and the Idea of a Transcontinental Nation* (Montreal and Kingston: McGill-/een's University Press, 2009).

5. *Glasgow International Exhibition, 1901: Official Guide* (Glasgow: Charles P. Watson, 1901), 30–31.

6. W.H. Hay, as quoted in William Saunders, "Appendix to the Report of the Minister of Agriculture: Experimental Farms Reports for 1901," *Sessional Paper* no. 16 (Ottawa, 1902), 78–79. Records of the Semiarid Prairie Agricultural Research Centre, Swift Current, SK.

7. Edward Said, *Culture and Imperialism* (London: Vintage Books, 1994), 15.

Tangential Tableau
Reworking Canadian Content
Anique Jordan

When I started writing this essay, I collected bits of conversations, journal entries, and scribbled thoughts, trying to find a way to make sense of my Black woman self in multiple spaces: within the institution of the art gallery, within this country on Indigenous land, and within this moment of nationally acknowledging Canada's colonial legacy. All these bodies exist: the institution, the state, and its party (Canada's 150th).

I, however, have to contend with the reality that in order for my body to simultaneously exist I would have to invent it, repeatedly. All of my recent artwork has been working through this idea and asking: What does it take for a Black person to survive in this country? And why, despite our survival, does the continued absence of our bodies in Canadian history, archives, and art galleries persist? What does an artist create from these conditions? It's the musing through these questions that produced the fragments of this work. They are unanswerable and can only be read by piecing them together through the same toiling that created them. These fragments, by their nature, necessarily disrupt the idea of linear time, of history as a singular story, and of Canada as a completed project. The pieces become more important than the whole.

1. **the body**
   The Institution
   The State
   And its Party

2. Blackness and Canadian-ness seem to be at odds.
   If I am Black, I am not Canadian.
   If I am Canadian, I am not Black.
   When I deliberately join these identities, I am uneasy.

3. I have always had a distinctly immigrant experience, despite being born Canadian. This may not come as insight for many Canadians for whom a white Anglo-Saxon identity is foreign. For those of us who, at first glance, are made out to be excluded from and void of Canadian-ness, we become tropes in a country for which our identities are employed only as strategies to brand a nation. We are equally the "culture" that multiculturalism remembers to celebrate at the times of anniversaries and parades as we are the bodies that disproportionately fill child welfare and penitentiary systems.

4. Canada, what are we marking?

5. Last year I created a series of photographs depicting the elder women in my family uniformed in regalia from the war of 1812. At the opening night of the exhibition a young Black woman approached me. She said she couldn't understand the images. She thought she saw white men, then men. She couldn't make sense of an image that felt so impossible to her: how could a Black woman be a Canadian hero?

6. I tell you, we are so accustomed to seeing ourselves displayed in some form of human extreme, or void of humanity in its entirety. The anger I feel about this is real: forced to make my humanity an exception.

7. Over Christmas, my cousins (who are white) are speaking to their mother about books of recipes their great-grandmother left for them. I turn to my mother (who is Black) and ask, "Do we have any books of recipes?" She replies, "We don't write down recipes." I have to shake this out of my body and remember again how insidious the colonial project is. Some archives are written, some are held in the body, and some in the land.

8. **The Institution**
   The State
   And its Party
   the body

9. Blackness and the Gallery seem to be at odds
   If I am Black, I am invisible or
   I am a Negro slave or
   I am an institutional threat or
   I am a security code or
   I am woefully diggin', diggin' bruk nails an all, teet mash up from grindin'
   Into the archives to find one
   Whose identity is not yet taxonomized
   Who I may call an auntie.
   When I deliberately join these identities, I am uneasy.

10. "Wen ya' miss me, I gone." There are real consequences for being unseen. Unseen people can disappear and be murdered and forgotten and forced to write essays with their invisible thread that only their children can decipher.

11. I have a question cycling in my head: How do we hold this institution accountable? Not solely by relying on the critiques its artists raise, but perhaps by recognizing its colonial foundations, or perhaps by openly acknowledging its inability to declare innocence.

12. What does it mean to create in this space?

13. . . . at this moment we are critiquing the Canadian state while replicating its power through the maintenance of an exclusive order and hanging the paintings of many, many, many white men.

14. **The State**
And its Party
the body
The Institution

15. iii. The cartographer says
no—
What I do is science. I show
the earth as it is, without bias.
I never fall in love. I never get involved
with the muddy affairs of land.
Too much passion unsteadies the hand.
I aim to show the full
of a place in just a glance

iv.
The rastaman thinks, draw me a map of what you see
then I will draw a map of what you never see
and guess me whose map will be bigger than whose?
Guess me whose map will tell the larger truth[1]

16. I think about the ways colonialism, slavery, and the events that continue to interrupt the lives of Indigenous and Black people recycle themselves in intimate relationships. We sit together, Black woman and Indigenous woman, brought to friendship in part seeking refuge in each other, in part learning to read the map.

17. Unburied: Canadian past, British imperialism, colonial legacy, the Dominion, the division of land.

18. "Cookies, cookies," said Sally.
"One for Dick and one for Jane.
One for me and one for Spot."[2]

19. *Where* are you from?
Canada.
No, where are *you* from?
Canada. I was born in Canada.
No, where are you *from* from?
Oooh!
Well my mother is from the Caribbean... my aunties are too
and I spent some early years in Brooklyn but further to that
I'm not sure... oh! but I know someone was enslaved in
the US and I did this ancestry thing and found out we are from
Nigeria... but... I'm not sure, cause that's just the Internet.

20. Rock, paper, scissors. Rock, paper, scissors. (1) Celebrating the process of reconciliation while (2) Celebrating the institution that warranted the need to reconcile to begin with. Rock, paper, scissors. Rock, paper, scissors. Which hand wins? Best 2 out of 3.

21. They don't mind that she still lives. They have already carved out her tongue.

22. The critiques surrounding Canada and Canada 150 are not new. Activists, scholars, artists, mothers, community workers, young people have always spoken back to the state, have always created alternatives to its colossal power, have always sought to imagine a different future. And now, to create artwork, to speak, to write and critique with state sponsorship (i.e., Canada 150 $$$), I question: have our survival strategies become commercial property of the state?

23. Canada™

24. What will be done with the 150th anniversaries of the births of these movements and activations?
- Black Lives Matter
- Idle No More
- No One Is Illegal
- Missing and Murdered Indigenous Women
- Black Women's Collective
- Yes Yes Y'all
- Sister Vision Press
- Blockorama
- Contrast Newspaper
- Watah Theatre
- Black Action Defence Committee (BADC)
- Glad Day Bookshop
- ...

25. The spaces that enable our survival are rendered dangerous, and condemned; our strategies of survival are interpreted as threats; and so, to you, leaders, trailblazers, and activists listed above, in 150 years, we might still need you, so today, I thank you for the work you do.

26. **And its Party**
the body
The Institution
The State

27. Blackness and Canadian-ness seem to be at odds.
If I am Black, I'm not Canadian.
If I am Canadian, I am not Black.
When I deliberately join these identities, I am uneasy.

28. …

Anique Jordan is a transdisciplinary artist, educator, activist, and social entrepreneur. A member of the Every. Now. Then. *curatorial team, she is also the executive director of Whippersnapper Gallery and lives in Toronto.*

NOTES

1. Kei Miller, *The Cartographer Tries to Map a Way to Zion* (Manchester: Carcanet, 2014), 18–19.

2. William S. Gray and Zerna Sharp, *Dick and Jane* (Glenview: Scott, Foresman and Company, 1934).
Dick and Jane are the main characters from a popular children's book series written by William S. Gray and Zerna Sharp in the 1930s. The books depict the everyday mischief of a white suburban family through the stories of Dick, Jane, Sally, and their dog, Spot. Indigenous artist Alex Janvier writes about his experience of language in residential school: "I didn't understand English or French. Much of what we learned was senseless. We learned about Dick and Jane."
I remember this children's book series from my childhood, found in many primary schools across the Caribbean. As a child I had a stuffed animal called Spot. My early writing as a child was based on characters like Dick and Jane, imagining that only white children could have stories written about them.

Exhibition

Published in conjunction with the exhibition
Every. Now. Then: Reframing Nationhood
Art Gallery of Ontario
Toronto, Ontario, Canada
June 29, 2017–February 18, 2018

Every. Now. Then: Reframing Nationhood is organized by the Art Gallery of Ontario. This project is supported by government partners Ontario 150, the Government of Canada, and the Canada Council for the Arts.

Art Gallery of Ontario
317 Dundas Street West
Toronto, Ontario M5T 1G4
Canada
www.ago.ca

CURATED BY
Andrew Hunter with
Anique Jordan and
Quill Christie-Peters

PROJECT MANAGER
Hillary Taylor

ASSISTANT DIRECTOR,
INTERPRETATION AND VISITOR RESEARCH
Keri Ryan

INTERPRETIVE PLANNER
Laura Robb

CURATORIAL ADMINISTRATIVE ASSISTANT
Donna Austria

EDITORS
Gina Badger
Amy Lam

DESIGNERS
Kristina Ljubanovic
Evelina Petrauskas

GRAPHIC PRODUCTION COORDINATOR
Malene Hjørngaard

CONSERVATION
Sherry Phillips
Joan Weir
Katharine Whitman
Meaghan Monaghan
Sjoukje van der Laan
John Williams

COLLECTIONS MANAGEMENT
Cindy Brouse
Jerry Drozdowsky
Tim Hardacre
Joel Herman
Dale Mahar
Curtis Strilchuk

MEDIA PRODUCTION AND INSTALLATION
Matthew Scott
Danny Winchester

LOGISTICS AND ART SERVICES
Scott Cameron
Corinne Carlson
Patric Colosimo
Brian Davis
Randal Fedje
Brian Groombridge
Roland Hardy
Iain Hoadley
Matthew Janisse
Ruth Jones
David Kinsman
Charles Kettle
Jason Laudadio
Alison Lindsay
Paul Mathiesen
Ben Oakley
John O'Leary
Jacques Oule
Angelo Pedari
Brent Roe
Sonia Sakamoto-Jog
Sabine Schaefer
Julie Seddon
Cecil Stein
Craig Whiteside
Darin Yorston
Tanya Zhilinsky

Publication

The Art Gallery of Ontario is partially funded by the Ontario Ministry of Culture. Additional operating support is received from the City of Toronto, the Department of Canadian Heritage and the Canada Council for the Arts.

Contemporary programming at the Art Gallery of Ontario is supported by

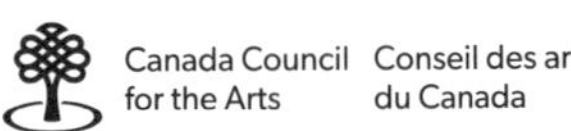

Printed and bound in Canada
10 9 8 7 6 5 4 3 2 1

Library and Archives Canada Cataloguing in Publication

Every. Now. Then : reframing nationhood / edited by Andrew Hunter.

Curated by Andrew Hunter with Anique Jordan and Quill Christie-Peters.
ISBN 978-1-894243-95-7 (softcover)

1. Art, Canadian—21st century—Exhibitions. 2. Canada—In art—Exhibitions. I. Hunter, Andrew, 1963–, editor, organizer II. Art Gallery of Ontario, issuing body, host institution

N6545.6E94 2017   709.71074'713541   C2017-902778-6

EDITED BY
Andrew Hunter

MANAGING EDITOR
Jim Shedden

PRODUCTION EDITOR
Gina Badger

MANUSCRIPT EDITOR
Mosa McNeilly

COPY EDITOR
Amy Lam

RESEARCHERS
Quill Christie-Peters
Anique Jordan
Laura Robb

PHOTOGRAPHY
Craig Boyko
Ian Lefebvre
Dean Tomlinson
Sean Weaver

RIGHTS AND REPRODUCTION
Jill Offenbeck

PROOFREADER
Judy Phillips

DESIGN
The Office of Gilbert Li

PRE-PRESS
Type A Print Inc.

PRINTING AND BINDING
Friesens, Canada

With the exception of those listed below, texts in the "Works" section of this book are the artists' own words, extracted and edited from interviews conducted in winter and spring 2017 by Laura Robb, with Anique Jordan and Andrew Hunter.

PAGE 16
Saimaiyu Akesuk: from an unpublished interview with Pat Fehely, 2014.

PAGE 40
Robert Houle: from "A Transatlantic Return Home Through the Magic of Art," in *Robert Houle's Paris/Ojibwa* (Peterborough: Art Gallery of Peterborough, 2011).

PAGE 44
Myung-Sun Kim: artist's text, unpublished, 2017.

PAGE 52
Esmaa Mohamoud: adapted from an interview by Anupa Mistry, "Sports Culture is the Catalyst for Esmaa Mohamoud's Art," *The Fader,* March 31, 2016, available online.

PAGE 54
Norval Morrisseau: adapted from interviews with Christopher Hume, "Morrisseau's New Colours Dazzle," *Toronto Star,* May 7, 1991, and Jennifer McCauley, "Debassige Presents an Eagle Feather to Idol: Internationally acclaimed artist Morrisseau," *Manitoulin Expositor,* September 29, 1999, available online.

PAGE 66
Curtis Talwst Santiago: from an interview by JZ, "An Interview with Talwst," *Tussle,* April 22, 2015, available online.

PAGE 78
Lawrence Paul Yuxweluptun: quoted in Christina Ritchie, "On a Good Day: Lawrence Paul Yuxweluptun Stands his Ground," *Canadian Art,* March 14, 2014, available online.

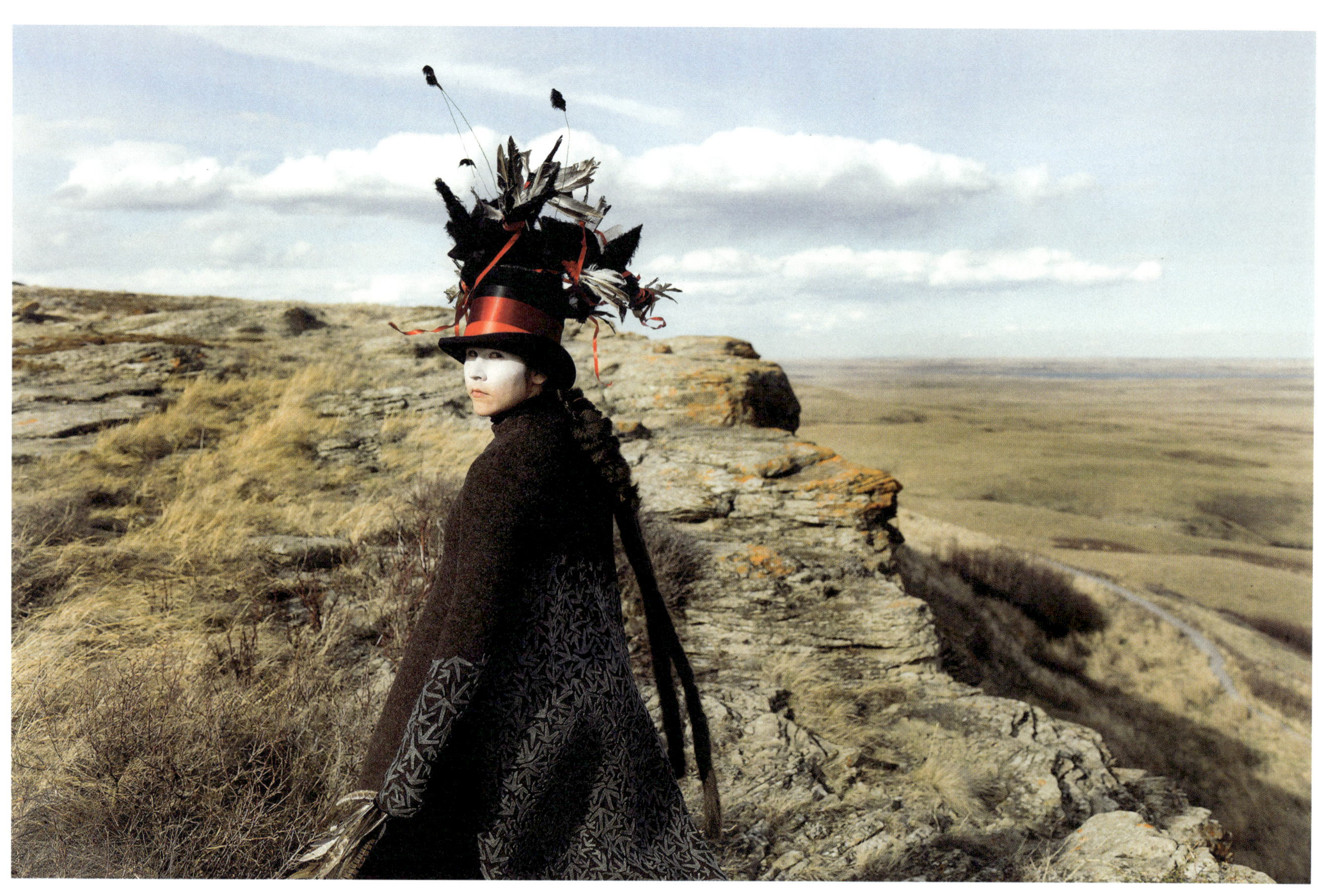

Meryl McMaster
Edge of a Moment, 2017
Inkjet print, 154.2 × 239.7 cm
Courtesy of the artist and Katzman Contemporary
Photo by the artist
at Head-Smashed-In Buffalo Jump, Alberta